MINUTE
GUIDE TO
1-2-3

Jenna Howard

alpha
books

A Division of Macmillan Computer Publishing

201 West 103rd Street, Indianapolis, Indiana 46290 USA

©1994 by Alpha Books

International Standard Book Number: 1-56761-408-6
Library of Congress Catalog Card Number: 93-73707

96   95   94   8   7   6   5   4   3   2   1

Interpretation of the printing code: the rightmost number of the first series of numbers is the year of the book's printing; the rightmost number of the second series of numbers is the number of the book's printing. For example, a printing code of 94-1 shows that the first printing of the book occurred in 1994.

Printed in the United States of America

Screen reproductions in this book were created by means of the program Collage Plus from Inner Media, Inc., Hollis, NH.

Publisher: Marie Butler-Knight
Managing Editor: Elizabeth Keaffaber
Product Development Manager: Faithe Wempen
Acquisitions Manager: Barry Pruett
Manuscript Editor: Audra Gable
Book Designer: Barbara Webster
Indexer: Bronte Davis
Production: Gary Adair, Brad Chinn, Kim Cofer, Mark Enochs, Stephanie Gregory, Jenny Kucera, Beth Rago, Bobbi Satterfield, Marc Shecter, Kris Simmons, Greg Simsic, Carol Stamile, Robert Wolf

Special thanks to Christopher Denny for ensuring the technical accuracy of this book.

Contents

Introduction

Suppose you walked into work this morning and found Lotus 1-2-3 on your desk. A note is stuck to the box: "We need a budget report for the upcoming meeting. See what you can do." Now what?

You could wade through the manuals that came with the program to find out how to perform a specific task, but that might take awhile, and it may tell you more than you want to know. You need a practical guide, one that will tell you exactly how to create and print the worksheets, reports, and graphs you need for the meeting.

Welcome to the 10 Minute Guide to 1-2-3!

Because most people don't have the luxury of sitting down uninterrupted for hours at a time to learn 1-2-3, this 10 Minute Guide does not attempt to teach everything about the program. Instead, it focuses on the most often-used features. Each feature is covered in a single self-contained lesson, which is designed to take 10 minutes or less to complete.

This 10 Minute Guide teaches you about the program without relying on technical jargon. With straightforward, easy-to-follow explanations and numbered lists that tell you what keys to press and what options to select, the *10 Minute Guide to 1-2-3* makes learning the program quick and easy.

How to Use This Book

The *10 Minute Guide to 1-2-3* consists of a series of lessons ranging from basic startup to a few more advanced features. If this is your first encounter with 1-2-3, you should probably work through lessons 1 through 17 in order. They lead you through the process of creating, editing, and printing a spreadsheet. The remaining lessons tell you how to use the more advanced features to create graphics and databases.

If 1-2-3 has not been installed on your computer, consult the inside front cover for installation steps.

Conventions Used in This Book

The following icons have been added throughout the book to help you find your way around:

Timesaver Tip icons offer shortcuts and hints for using the program efficiently.

Plain English icons define new terms.

Panic Button icons appear where new users often run into trouble.

The following conventions have been used to clarify the steps you must perform.

On-screen text	Any text that appears on-screen is shown in bold.
What you type	The information you type appears in bold and color.

Commands and Options	The names of menus, commands, buttons, and dialog boxes are shown with the first letter capitalized for easy recognition.
Main menu selections	If you must open the main menu (by pressing the / key) to choose a command, the command is preceded by a / mark, as in /File.
Key+Key combinations	In many cases, you must press a two-key combination in order to enter a command. For example, if the text says "Press Alt+X," you do so by holding down the first key while pressing the second key.

For Further Reference . . .

If you want a more detailed guide to using Lotus 1-2-3, we suggest *The Complete Idiot's Guide to 1-2-3* by Peter Aitken.

Acknowledgments

Once again, I've enjoyed working with the development team at Alpha Books. Special thanks to publisher Marie Butler-Knight for asking me to write this book, and to Faithe Wempen, Liz Keaffaber, and Audra Gable for their excellent editorial work.

Lesson

Starting and Exiting Lotus 1-2-3

In this lesson, you will learn how to start Lotus 1-2-3, turn Wysiwyg on and off, and exit 1-2-3.

The Lotus 1-2-3 program must be installed correctly on your hard disk before you can begin your work. If you have not yet installed 1-2-3, see the inside front cover for installation instructions.

Starting 1-2-3

Follow these steps to start 1-2-3 from your hard disk:

1. Make sure you are at the DOS prompt where you installed 1-2-3 (for example, C: or D:).

2. To move to the 1-2-3 Release 4 directory, where you installed 1-2-3 software, type **CD\123R4D** and press Enter.

3. Type **123** and press Enter. You will briefly see a logo screen, showing your name and your organization's name, which you entered the first time you used Install. The work area appears on-screen (see Figure 1.1).

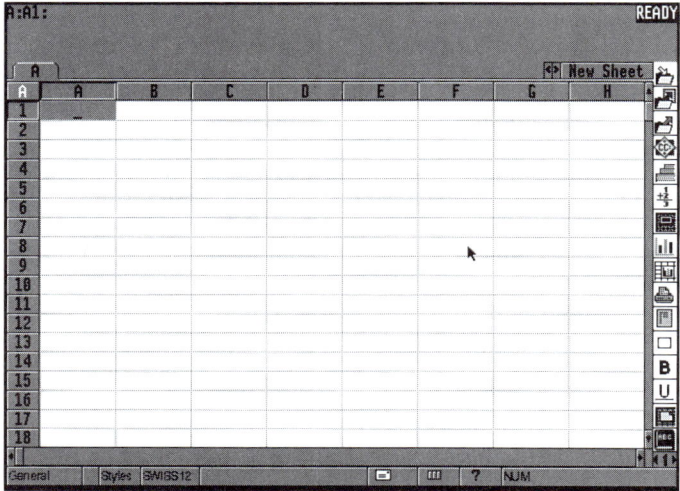

Figure 1.1   Lotus 1-2-3's initial work area.

It Won't Work   If 1-2-3 encounters problems at startup, an error message (such as **Bad command or filename**) will appear. Make sure you followed the "Starting 1-2-3" steps correctly; you could try these steps again. If you get the same error message, try reinstalling 1-2-3, following the instructions on the inside front cover of this book.

Retrieving a File at Startup

You can retrieve a worksheet file at the same time you are starting 1-2-3, which will save you several steps during a 1-2-3 work session.

To retrieve a file at startup, type 123 followed by a space, and then type – (hyphen) and the letter W (for worksheet), followed by the name of a worksheet file. For

instance, you would type 123 -wchecks and press Enter to
retrieve a file named CHECKS.WK3 in the 1-2-3 default
directory.

> **Detailed Directions**   If the worksheet file you
> want to retrieve is on a separate disk (or in a
> different directory), you can also type a *path* in
> front of the file name to tell 1-2-3 where to look for
> the worksheet. To retrieve CHECKS.WK3 from a disk in
> drive A, for example, type 123 -wa:\checks and then
> press Enter.

Alternate Start from Windows

You can start 1-2-3 from Windows if you've added the 1-2-3
icon to the Windows desktop. Double-click the icon (point
to it with the mouse pointer and press and release the left
mouse button twice quickly). If you don't have a 1-2-3 icon
set up in Windows, refer to 1-2-3 documentation for the
steps for creating the icon.

Turning Wysiwyg On and Off

WYSIWYG (pronounced "wizzy-wig") is a fun word that
stands for "What-You-See-Is-What-You-Get." Wysiwyg is also
the name for one of 1-2-3's special programs. In this case,
Wysiwyg lets you print exactly what you see on your screen.
To demonstrate what it is and how useful it can be, we
created the figures in this book with 1-2-3 in *Wysiwyg mode*.
If you have the right video card and monitor, Wysiwyg will
start up automatically. Figure 1.1 shows the initial 1-2-3
display in Wysiwyg mode.

Follow these steps to remove or attach Wysiwyg.

1. Press **Alt+F10** to activate the Add-In menu shown in
Figure 1.2.

Add-In menu

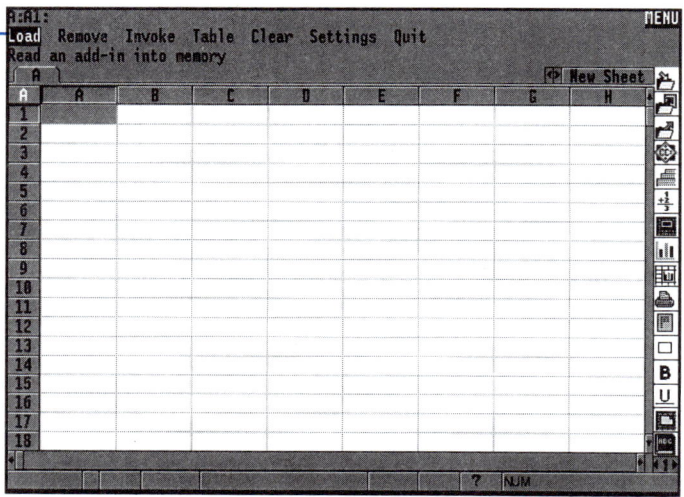

Figure 1.2 The Add-In menu.

2. Use the arrow keys or the mouse to select Remove or Load.

3. From the list of add-ins on-screen, select Wysiwyg. If you want to see additional choices, press →.

4. Press Enter once to remove Wysiwyg or twice to load it.

5. Select Quit. 1-2-3 returns you to READY mode.

For more information on using Wysiwyg, see Lesson 19.

Exiting Lotus 1-2-3

Follow these instructions to end your work session and exit Lotus 1-2-3.

1. Press / (slash) or move the mouse pointer into the Control Panel (at the top of the screen) to display the 1-2-3 main menu. This menu, described in Lesson 3, contains commands you'll use as you work in 1-2-3.

2. Select Quit.

3. If 1-2-3 asks if you want to save a worksheet, select No for now. For details on saving a worksheet and exiting, see Lesson 7.

4. Select Yes to end the session. 1-2-3 returns you to the DOS prompt if you started 1-2-3 from DOS, or to the Windows desktop if you started 1-2-3 from Windows.

Shortcuts!   1-2-3 allows you to press the first letter of each command to select it (for example, press Q for Quit, Y for Yes, and so on). You can also select a command by using the cursor arrows to highlight it, and then pressing Enter.

I Only Want to Leave for a Moment
Release 4 has a special feature that lets you return to the DOS prompt without having to leave 1-2-3. So if you want to go to DOS but leave 1-2-3 running, use the /Tools DOS command. Type exit at the DOS prompt to return to 1-2-3.

In this lesson, you learned how to start Lotus 1-2-3 from DOS or Windows, turn Wysiwyg on and off, retrieve an application at startup, and exit Lotus 1-2-3. In Lesson 2, you will learn about basic screen elements and about moving around 1-2-3 with the keyboard and mouse.

Lesson

Worksheet Basics

2

In this lesson you'll learn about 1-2-3 worksheet structure, and how to move around in a worksheet using the keyboard and the mouse.

1-2-3's Work Area

Have you ever done any bookkeeping? If so, you may have used some of the green columnar paper from an accountant's pad. 1-2-3's work area is organized into columns and rows somewhat like that accounting paper. This arrangement (called a *worksheet*) makes it easy to organize your data. (Remember that columns run up and down, while rows run across the work area.)

Cells and Addresses

In all spreadsheet software, a *cell* is the basic unit of a worksheet; it allows you to store data, and always refers to the intersection of one *column* and one *row*. Figure 2.1 shows the spreadsheet cursor, called a *cell pointer*, located at the intersection of column D and row 12. The cell address is D12. When giving a cell address, refer to the column (in this case D) and then the row (in this case 12). The cell where the cell pointer is located is called the *active cell*.

Row Column Cell is intersection of row and column.

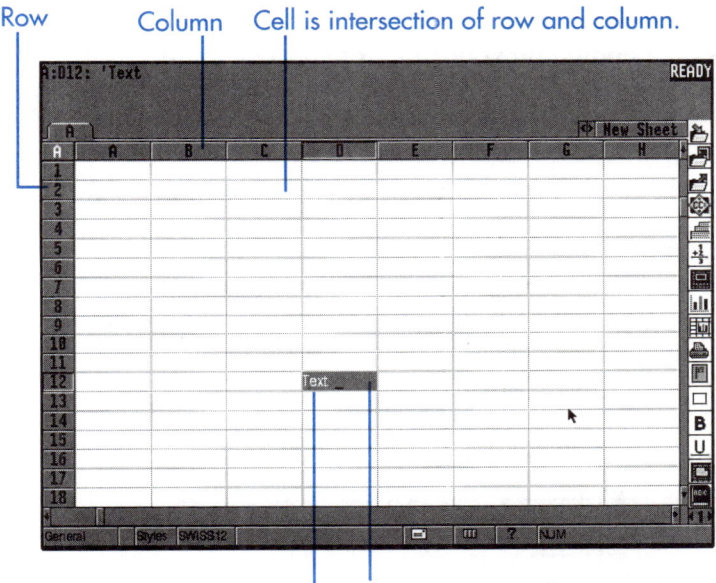

Shaded block is the cell pointer. Cell on which cell pointer rests
is the active cell.

Figure 2.1 The 1-2-3 work area is composed of intersecting
rows and columns, which form cells.

How do you know which letters and numbers represent
which columns and rows? Look at the top of 1-2-3's screen:
the column letter where the cell pointer sits is highlighted.
(In 1-2-3 WYSIWYG mode, a highlighted column letter looks
like a pressed button.) 1-2-3 boasts 256 columns, lettered
from A to IV.

At the left edge of the work area is a line that numbers
the worksheet's rows from 1 to 8,192 (though of course they
won't fit on your screen all at once). The highlighted row
number marks the row where the cell pointer is located.

The exact number of cells displayed at any given time varies depending on your monitor and video mode, but you'll probably see at least cells A1 through H18. In the next lesson, you'll learn how to move all around this work area.

Moving Around the Worksheet

Each worksheet is much too large to fit on-screen at once. As you view your worksheet, you can see only about 8 columns and 18 rows. Figure 2.2 shows what the whole worksheet looks like in relationship to what you see on-screen.

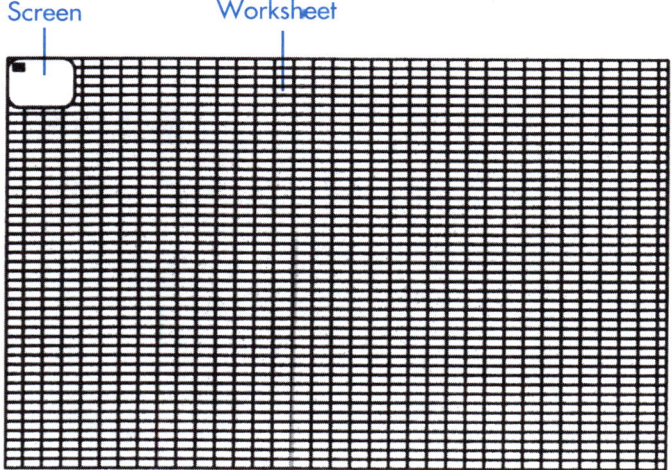

Figure 2.2   The worksheet area displayed on-screen is a small portion of the worksheet.

To view areas of the worksheet other than what is currently displayed on-screen, you can use either the keyboard or the mouse.

Moving Around with the Keyboard

The simplest way to move the cell pointer with the keyboard is to press your keyboard's arrow keys. They move the cell pointer one cell in the indicated direction. If the cell pointer is already at the edge of the screen, pressing the arrow key scrolls the display one cell in that direction.

Table 2.1 shows these and other keys you can use to move around the worksheet.

Sheet to Sheet? The keys in Table 2.1 will move the cell pointer around on a single sheet. You'll learn to move from one worksheet or file to another later in this book.

Table 2.1   Using Keys to Move the Cell Pointer

Press	To move cell pointer
← or →	Left or right one column.
↑ or ↓	Up or down one row.
Ctrl+← or Shift+Tab	Left one screen.
Ctrl+→ or Tab	Right one screen.
End, Home	To the bottom right corner of the worksheet's active area.
Home	To cell A1, if column A is not hidden and worksheet titles are not set.
PgUp or PgDn	Up or down one screen.

Moving Around with the Mouse

You can also move around with a mouse as well as a keyboard. To use a mouse, you'll need to be familiar with these terms:

Point   To move the mouse so the pointer is over the cell or menu option you want to select.

Click   To point to the cell or option you want, and press and release the left mouse button.

Double-click   To point to the cell or option you want, and press and release the left mouse button twice quickly.

Drag   To place the mouse pointer at the point on-screen where you want your selection to begin, press and hold the left mouse button, and then move the mouse pointer until the group of cells you want is highlighted. Then release the mouse button.

Just click on the cell you want if it's in view. If it's not in view, use the scroll bars to scroll to the area of the worksheet that contains the cell you want to work with. Then click on the cell to select it. Scroll bars are shown in Figure 2.3.

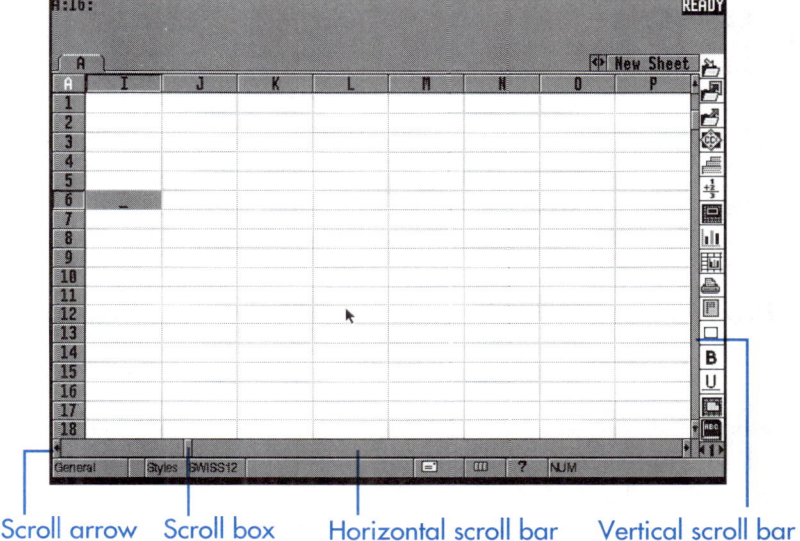

Scroll arrow   Scroll box   Horizontal scroll bar   Vertical scroll bar

Figure 2.3 Scroll bars enable you to move around in a worksheet using the mouse.

To use scroll bars:

- Click once on a scroll arrow at the end of the scroll bar to scroll incrementally in the direction of the arrow. Hold down the mouse button to scroll continuously.

- Drag the scroll box along the scroll bar to the area of the worksheet you want to view. For example, to move to the middle of the worksheet, drag the scroll box to the middle of the scroll bar.

- Click once inside the scroll bar, on either side of the scroll box, to move the view one screenful at a time in that direction.

In this lesson, you learned about rows, columns, and cells, and you learned how to move around in a worksheet. In the next lesson, you'll learn about the various screen elements that help you control your worksheet.

Lesson 3

The 1-2-3 Controls

In this lesson, you'll learn about the various controls that 1-2-3 provides to help you manage a worksheet.

Everything you need to work with 1-2-3—menus, commands, work area, and mode indicators—you will find ready and waiting on the 1-2-3 screen. All the elements are right there! You learned about the work area in Lesson 2; now let's take a look at the various controls and indicators that surround it.

The Control Panel

Look at the top of your 1-2-3 screen, and you'll see the *control panel*. The control panel's main purpose is to display menus of commands for you to select from. To display the menus, simply press the slash key (/) or move the mouse pointer to the top of the screen. When you do, menus appear, as in Figure 3.1.

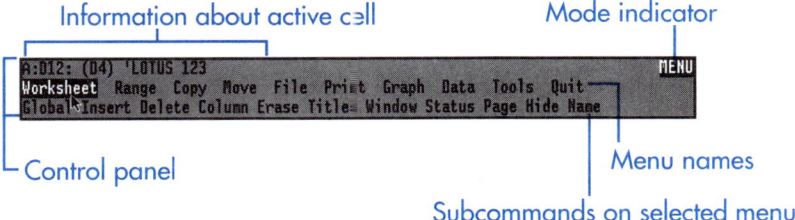

Figure 3.1 The 1-2-3 control panel's most prominent feature is the menu system.

The first line of the control panel is not used by the menu system. Instead, it displays the following information about the current cell:

Address: A:C27 is the address, for instance, of the cell in worksheet A at the intersection of column C and row 27.

Format: If the cell is to be formatted in a way that differs from the default cell format, this choice controls the way 1-2-3 displays data in the cell.

Protection status: Lets you know whether you can make changes to the cell when worksheet protection is on.

Column width: If you have changed the default column width, this area shows the number of characters 1-2-3 will display in the cell.

Entry: This area shows the actual data stored in the cell.

Mode indicator: Located at the far right of the first line of the control panel, the mode indicator tells you the *mode*, or state, in which 1-2-3 is currently running. (Table 3.1 lists the 1-2-3 modes.) After you press / (slash), for example, 1-2-3 is in MENU mode, and the mode indicator reads MENU.

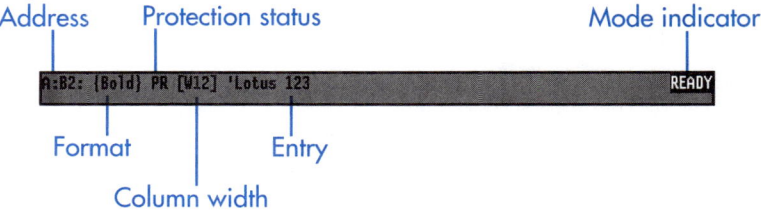

Figure 3.2   The first line of the control panel offers several pieces of information about the active cell.

The second line of the control panel shows you one of these three items:

- The Main menu if you press / (slash) or < (the less than symbol).

- The current entry when you enter or edit data.

- The *prompts* (requests for information) that 1-2-3 needs to complete a command.

When 1-2-3 is in MENU mode, the third line of the control panel displays either a description of the highlighted command or a list of subcommands. When 1-2-3 is in FILES or NAMES mode, the third line shows a list of files or names.

Mode Indicators

Whenever you are working with 1-2-3, mode indicators give you a message describing what's going on. For example, when you type a number or formula into a cell, the mode indicator VALUE appears in the upper right corner of the screen. 1-2-3's mode indicators are listed in Table 3.1.

Table 3.1   Mode Indicators in 1-2-3 Release 4

Mode	Description
EDIT	You're editing the contents of a cell.
ERROR	An error has resulted from a formula or operation; to remove this indicator, press Esc or Enter.
FILES	1-2-3 waits for you to select a file name.
FIND	1-2-3 is searching a database.
HELP	1-2-3 is displaying a Help screen.
LABEL	You are typing text (i.e., a *label*) into a cell.

Mode	Description
MENU	1-2-3 shows you a menu and waits for you to select an option.
NAMES	1-2-3 displays a list of range names and waits for you to select one.
POINT	You are selecting some connected cells (a *range*).
READY	1-2-3 waits for you to give a command or enter data into a cell.
SETTINGS	You have called up a dialog box.
STAT	The current screen is a STATUS screen.
VALUE	You are typing a number (i.e., *value*) or a formula into a cell.
WAIT	You must wait while 1-2-3 carries out a command.
WYSIWYG	1-2-3 is showing you what you'll get if you print.

The Status Bar

The status bar is the bottom line of the screen. It's a "live" status bar, in that it does more than just display information on the current settings of cells. If you have a mouse, you can click on some parts of the status bar to open *pick lists*, from which you can actually change cell settings.

Nothing Happens!   Not all parts of the status bar are live. Some parts, such as the status indicators, merely display information. If you click on an area of the status bar and nothing happens, you probably clicked on one of the "dead" areas.

On the left end of the status bar are buttons that enable you to change formats, line styles, and font types and sizes. When you click on any of these buttons, a pick list appears listing your options. Click on an option, or press Esc to close the list without picking.

The middle section of the status bar toggles between showing the date and time, the name of the current file, and the information (such as cell width) about the current cell. Clicking in this area simply switches among displays; the display is for information only.

Toward the right end are buttons that retrieve Email, switch SmartIcon palettes, and access Help. Click on these to activate them. On the far right are status indicators, another info-only display covered later in this lesson. Figure 3.3 shows what each part of the status bar is used for.

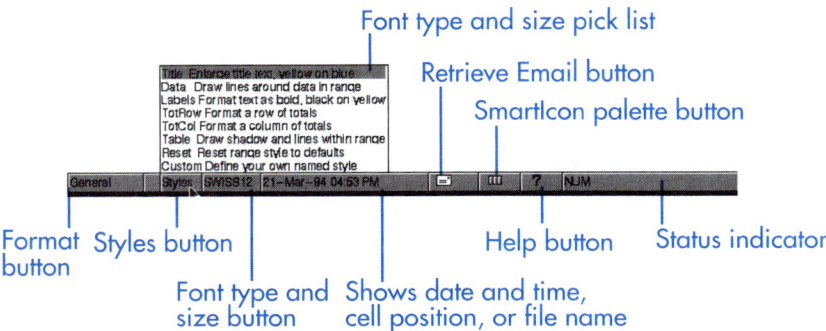

Figure 3.3   The status bar provides helpful information, and its buttons provide access to pick lists that help format cells quickly.

Selecting from a Status Bar Pick List

The "live" buttons on the left end of the status bar provide access to pick lists from which you can pick cell formatting. Here's how to use one:

1. Move the cell pointer to the cell you want to modify, or select a range of cells to modify. (You'll learn about selecting ranges of cells in Lesson 7.)

2. Click on the status bar button you want to use (for example, styles or fonts). A pick list of choices appears just above the status bar, as in Figure 3.3.

3. Click on the new setting you want.

The cell(s) changes to the new setting. Notice that the status bar displays the name of the new setting you chose.

Status Indicators

1-2-3 uses the right side of the status bar to display the file and clock indicator, and various status indicators (such as CAPS when the Caps Lock key is on). *Status indicators* let you know the type of operation 1-2-3 is performing. They also let you know when an error occurs, and the type of error it is. Table 3.2 shows the status indicators and their meanings.

Table 3.2   Status Indicators in 1-2-3 Release 4

Indicator	Meaning
CALC	Recalculate the worksheet.
CAP	The Caps Lock key is engaged.
CIRC	Correct a circular reference error (such as adding a total to a total).
CMD	A macro is running.
LEARN	1-2-3 is "learning" by recording a macro from your keystrokes.
END	You pressed End; press an arrow key to move the pointer.
FILE	You are in the process of moving between files.

continues

Table 3.2 Continued

Indicator	Meaning
GROUP	GROUP mode is in effect for this file.
MEM	Warning: your computer's memory is almost full.
NUM	The Num Lock key is engaged.
OVR	You are editing data in Overstrike mode.
PRT	1-2-3 is printing the current file.
RO	Read-Only; no changes to this file will be saved.
SCROLL	The Scroll Lock key is engaged.
STEP	A macro is running one step at a time.
ZOOM	You have a full-screen view of a worksheet window.

Removing Status Indicators You can remove a status indicator by pressing Esc or Enter; you'll return to the READY mode.

Customizing the 1-2-3 Screen

Sometimes the 1-2-3 screen may feel crowded to you. If so, you can do something about it. 1-2-3 gives you the option of displaying or not displaying the SmartIcons, Scroll bars, Worksheet tabs, and dialog boxes. To set the screen display:

1. Press / or move the mouse pointer to the control panel area to open the menus.

2. Press Enter to select Worksheet, and press Enter again to select Global. The Global Settings dialog box appears.

3. Press F2 or click anywhere on the Global settings dialog box. New buttons appear at the bottom of the dialog box, including the Default Settings button.

4. Click on the Default Settings button or Tab to it and press Enter. The Default Settings dialog box appears, as shown in Figure 3.4.

These options give you control over the screen's appearance.

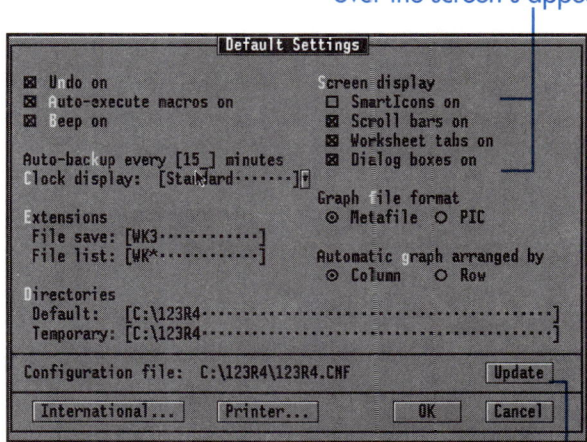

Click this button to put the new settings into effect.

Figure 3.4   The Default Settings dialog box.

5. Press F2 or click anywhere in the dialog box to edit the dialog box settings.

6. In the Screen display section of the dialog box, mark the options you want to be displayed. To mark or unmark an option, click on it or Tab to it and press the Spacebar. Check marks appear in the check boxes of those items you select; check marks are removed from items you deselect.

7. Click on the Update button in the lower right corner of the dialog box, or Tab to it and press Enter.

8. Press Esc several times to return to the 1-2-3 screen.

In this lesson, you learned about the control panel and the status bar, and how to configure the appearance of the 1-2-3 screen. In the next lesson, you'll learn how to use 1-2-3's menus and dialog boxes and how to get help.

Lesson

Using 1-2-3's Menus

In this lesson you'll learn how to operate 1-2-3's menu system, select commands, retrieve a file, and get help.

The Main Menu

The main menu appears at the top of the screen when you move the mouse pointer there or press /. From it, you select the commands and subcommands you want to execute.

Menu Selections A *menu* is a series of choices that 1-2-3 displays in the second line of the control panel. You select a command from a menu by highlighting it and pressing Enter, or by typing the first letter in the command's name.

Table 4.1 lists the main menu commands and gives a brief explanation of their functions:

Table 4.1 Main Menu Commands in 1-2-3

Command	Enables you to
Worksheet	Affect the whole worksheet.
Range	Select and work with a range of cells.
Copy	Copy a cell or range of cells.

continues

Table 4.1 Continued

Command	Enables you to
Move	Move a cell or range of cells.
File	Perform various operations on files.
Print	Print a range of cells or a whole worksheet.
Graph	Create or change a graph.
Data	Work with database features.
Tools	Check spelling, attach notes, and exit to DOS, among other functions.
Quit	End the work session.

Selecting Menu Commands

When 1-2-3's main menu first appears (see Figure 4.1), you'll see a list of the commands available to you. *Commands* tell 1-2-3 to perform such tasks as copying data, saving files, and printing your worksheet.

Subcommand The main menu does not have room to show every command, so many commands are grouped into logical categories (such as Worksheet) and placed as *subcommands* of a main menu command. Except that they do not appear on the main menu, subcommands are the same as commands.

Most commands on the main menu are actually headings for groups of subcommands; selecting a main menu command opens a list of other commands you can choose.

Main menu   Main menu commands   Subcommands for
                                          Worksheet menu

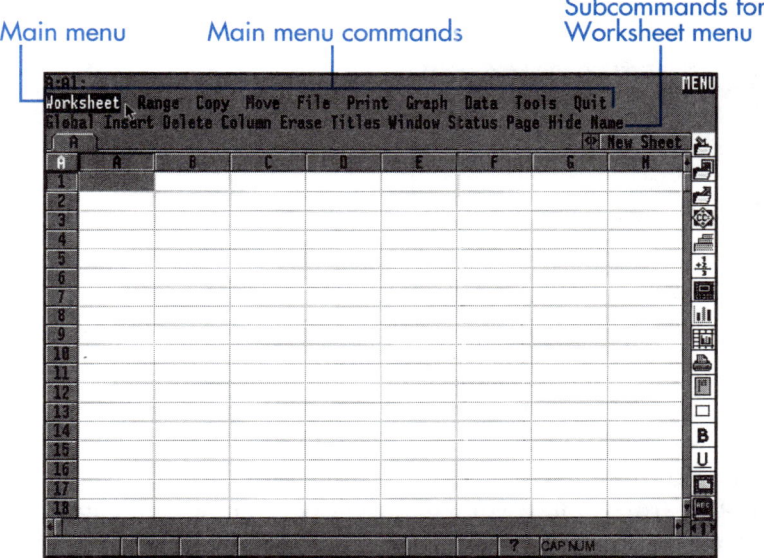

Figure 4.1 The 1-2-3 main menu.

The highlighted rectangle positioned on the Worksheet command (in Figure 4.1) is the *menu pointer*. When you move the mouse pointer over a command, the third line of the control panel displays either subcommands or information about the highlighted command.

To select a command from the menu using the mouse:

1. Move the mouse pointer into the control panel area.

2. When the main menu appears, click on the command you want.

To select a menu command from the menu with the keyboard:

1. Press the / (slash) key.

2. Use the arrow keys to move through the command list until the command you need is highlighted.

3. Press Enter.

Alternate Selection Method You can also select a command by pressing the first letter of its name on the keyboard.

The Right Slash When bringing up the main menu, be sure to use the / (slash) key, not the \ (backslash) key. If you make a mistake, return to the previous screen by pressing Esc, and press / (slash) to get the main menu.

From now on in this book, I'll assume that you know how to select commands. When you need to select a command from the main menu, it'll appear in this book with a slash in front of it. If you need to select a subcommmand after it, the subcommand name will follow. For instance, select /File Save means to select File from the main menu and then select the Save subcommand.

Entering Information

Sometimes a command you've selected requires that you type information in order to continue. For example, if you choose /File Save, you'll be asked to enter the name of the file you are saving. In this case, type in the path and the name of the worksheet. Don't put in an extension; 1-2-3 does that for you. Press Enter (or click the left mouse button), and press Esc repeatedly until you return to the Main menu.

Leaving a Trail Typing in a path tells 1-2-3 the drive and directory it should use to find your stored file. Your DOS manual can give you more details.

Dialog Boxes

Dialog boxes appear when Lotus needs more information about the function you are performing; they also display options available with the function. See Figure 4.2 for an example of a dialog box. To make a selection from a dialog box, follow these steps:

1. When a dialog box appears, press F2 to enter EDIT mode or click anywhere within the box.

2. Press Tab to move to the option you want to edit, or press the first letter of the name of the option. With the mouse, you simply click on the option name.

3. Using the arrow keys, highlight the option you want to edit and press the Spacebar to select it. Or click on the option with the mouse.

```
┌──────────────────── Wysiwyg Print Settings ────────────────────┐
│ Range(s): [·············]░ ░      Send output to: [Printer···]░ │
│                                   File name: [C:\123R4\*.ENC···]░│
│ Settings                                                        │
│  Beginning page:  [1·]            Layout                        │
│  Ending page:     [99]             Header: [··················] │
│  Start numbering: [1·]             Footer: [··················] │
│  Copies:          [1·]             Left border: [········]░ ░   │
│  ☐ Print worksheet frame           Top border: [········]░      │
│  ☐ Print grid lines                Compression type:  [None···]░│
│  ☐ Wait for paper change           Compression ratio: [10]      │
│                                    Page type:  [1:Letter······]░│
│                                     Height: [8.5in··]Width: [11in····]│
│ Margins                                                         │
│  Left  [8.5in···]Top:    [8.5in···] Units                       │
│  Right: [8.5in···]Bottom: [0.55in··]  ◉ Inches   ○ Millimeters  │
│              ┌── Press F2 or Click Dialog Box ──┐               │
└──────────────────────────────────────────────────────────────┘
```

Figure 4.2   An example of a dialog box.

Help!

At any time, you can press F1 (Help) or click on the Help icon on the status bar (the question mark) to see a Help screen with information about the part of the program you're using (see Figure 4.3). Notice the words that appear in a contrasting color (or a brighter intensity) within the current Help screen, and at the bottom of the screen. These stand for related topics on which you can also get Help. To select one of them, use the arrow keys to move to the topic you want, and press Enter. To exit Help, press the Esc key.

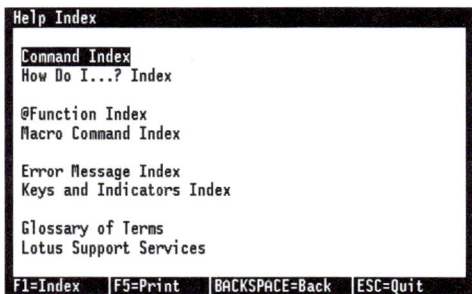

Figure 4.3   The 1-2-3 Help Screen.

In this lesson, you learned how to access 1-2-3's main menu, select menu commands, retrieve a file, and use the Help feature. In the next lesson, you will learn about using 1-2-3's SmartIcons to speed up routine operations.

Lesson

SmartIcons

This lesson shows you how you can perform routine steps quickly by using 1-2-3's SmartIcons.

SmartIcons help you make your spreadsheet look good with a minimum of fuss. You can format a range of cells with a special outline in the blink of an eye, make a heading bold and underlined with a click, or apply any of dozens of other formatting changes—all by clicking on a SmartIcon.

SmartIcons are the sixteen buttons that appear to the far right of the worksheet, as shown in Figure 5.1. Each button shows a graphic representation of a worksheet task, or gives you quick access to 1-2-3 commands. (Remember: if you want to access SmartIcons, the Icons add-in and the Wysiwyg add-in must be running. They were loaded by default if you installed 1-2-3 with an EGA or VGA monitor hooked up. If you don't see the SmartIcons at the right of your work area, see Lesson 10, "Working with Lotus 1-2-3's Add-Ins.")

Something's Missing If you have an EGA screen display card, you will see only 12 of the 16 icons shown in Figure 5.1. However, you can still gain access to the four additional icons and to other icons not currently visible. Read the section in this lesson titled "Customizing Your Palette."

SmartIcon palette

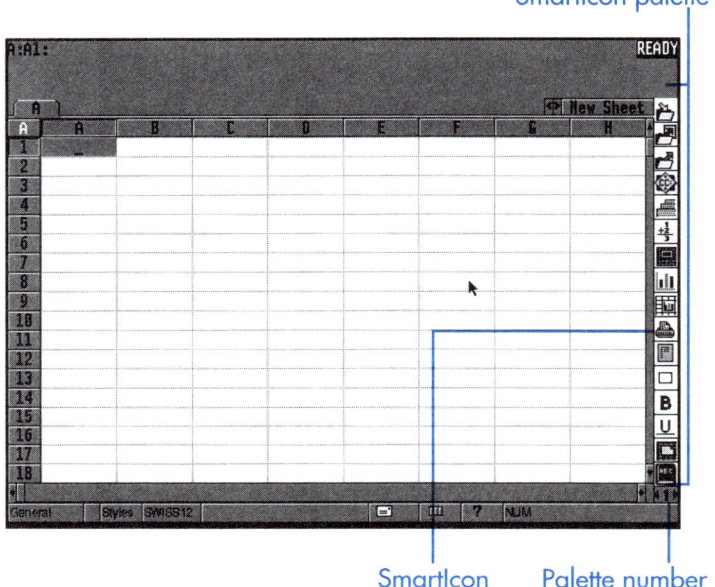

Figure 5.1   1-2-3's SmartIcons.

SmartIcon   Palette number

Getting to Know Lotus 1-2-3's SmartIcons

For convenience, SmartIcons are organized in *palettes*. You can switch among eight different palettes of powerful SmartIcons by clicking on the arrowheads on either side of the palette number, which is displayed at the bottom of the palette column. Or, you can pick a new palette from the pick list (shown in Figure 5.2) that appears when you click on the palette icon on the status bar (to the left of the question mark). Keyboard users can change palettes by pressing Ctrl+F10 and using the left and right arrow keys.

To see a description of any icon, just click and hold on the icon with the right mouse button. The description appears in the third line of 1-2-3's control panel. Table 5.1 gives you the functions of the SmartIcons presented on the start-up palette.

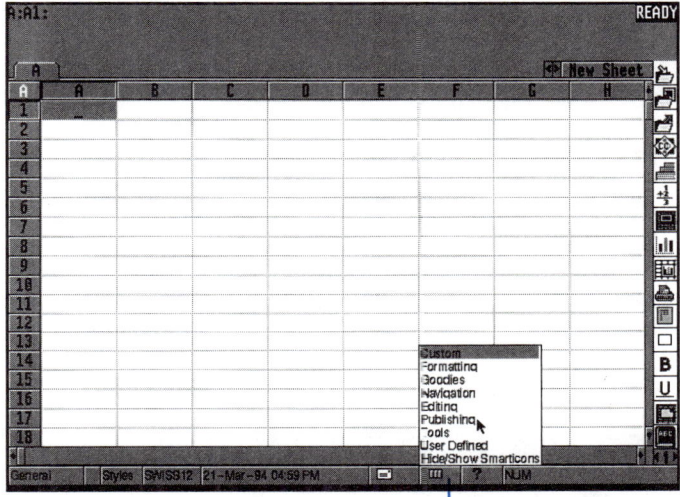

Click here to display pick
list of palettes.

Figure 5.2   Switching palettes using the status bar.

Custom Palette   The start-up palette is also
the *custom palette*, containing the most commonly
used icons from the other seven palettes. You can
customize the start-up palette by adding the icons
you use most often, or deleting those you no longer use.
The other seven palettes cannot be modified.

Table 5.1   The Start-Up SmartIcon Palette

Icon	Enables you to
	Save your worksheet to a disk.
	Replace your file with one from the disk.

continues

Table 5.1   Continued

Icon	Enables you to
	Read a file into memory after the current file.
	Send a message via cc:Mail.
	See three worksheets, stacked up.
	Calculate the sum of values in a range.
	Access the Version Manager.
	Create, edit, or display a graph.
	Add your graph to the worksheet.
	Print a selected range of cells.
	Print the previous (or a specified) range.
	Cycle through available outlines and shadows.
	Add boldface to (or remove it from) a range.
	Add single underlining to (or remove it from) data in a range.
	Attach a note to a cell.
	Spell-check the worksheet.

More About Smartlcons See the appendix at the end of the book for a chart containing all of the Lotus 1-2-3 Smartlcons.

Selecting Smartlcons

It's easy to use the mouse to select an icon to perform a task—you just click on the icon! Click on the arrows surrounding the SmartIcon palette number to move through the palettes.

It's a little more cumbersome to select an icon from a SmartIcon palette with the keyboard:

1. Press Ctrl+F10.

2. Press ← or → to select a SmartIcon palette.

3. Press ↑ or ↓ to select a SmartIcon.

4. Press Enter to activate the icon.

Customizing Your Palette

When you start 1-2-3 in WYSIWYG mode, palette 1 (the custom palette) appears with its set of specific SmartIcons. You can exchange icons on this palette with icons from other palettes. For example, here's how to replace SmartIcon 16 on palette 1 with an icon from the second palette (the double-underline icon):

1. Switch to icon palette 7.

2. Select the Add Icon SmartIcon .

3. Switch to palette 2 and select the icon that you want to add to the custom palette (in this case, the bottom icon, which is the double-underline icon).

1-2-3 will replace the bottom icon on the custom palette with the new icon, and return you to READY mode. 1-2-3 always adds the chosen icon to the bottom of the custom palette. If the palette is full, 1-2-3 replaces the last icon. If you don't want the last one replaced, remove the one you do want replaced first (see the next procedure).

> **Gone? Not!**   When you replace a SmartIcon, you aren't physically moving it. Instead, the SmartIcon you've chosen is copied from its home palette to the custom palette. If that palette is full, 1-2-3 replaces the bottom icon.

You can also remove icons from the custom palette. Here's how:

1. Select the icon palette 7.

2. Select the Del Icon SmartIcon . The start-up (custom) icon palette appears.

3. Click on the icon you want to remove. It is deleted.

In this lesson, you learned to use SmartIcons to speed up your work, as well as how to move between palettes and move SmartIcons to the start-up (custom) palette. In the next lesson you'll learn how to enter data.

Lesson

Entering Data

In this lesson, you will learn how to type labels and values in a worksheet.

Plan Before You Begin

There are many types of data that you can enter into a 1-2-3 worksheet, and many ways to use this data to create a worksheet. Some spreadsheets are far more effective than others, so it pays to plan before you start typing.

> **Data Types** You can enter dates, times, formulas, numbers, and text into 1-2-3 spread-sheets.

Suppose for a moment that you have a small stationery store business. You want to keep track of the fourth-quarter sales revenues by individual items sold. Later you will analyze and graph these figures.

On paper, you note that the months of October, November, and December will occupy your columns. You also note that names of each item category can occupy separate rows. Figure 6.1 shows the sample 1-2-3 spread-sheet.

Column labels

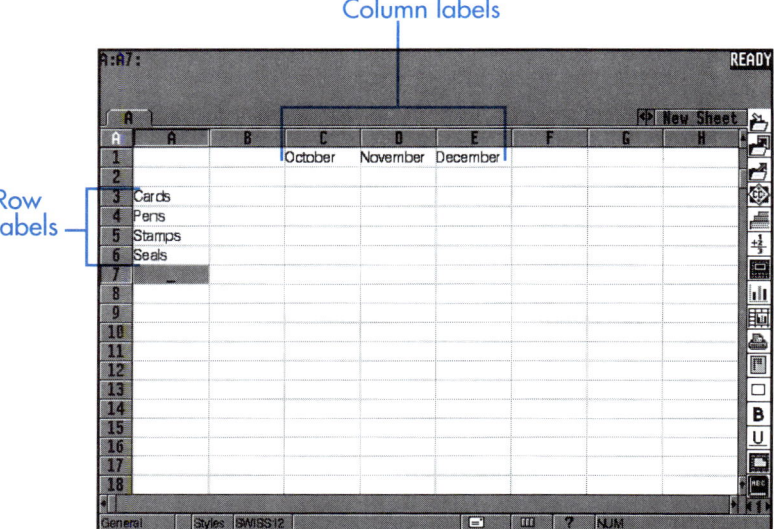

Figure 6.1   The sample stationery store spreadsheet with labels.

Typing Labels

It's easiest to begin a spreadsheet by typing in the labels. If you're following this business example, you could enter the column labels first, followed by the row labels.

Labels Are   In a spreadsheet program, a *label* is any text you type into a cell. Labels are distinguished from values (numeric entries), formulas (equations that perform operations on values), and functions (a shorthand for complex formulas).

Can't Enter Data   You cannot enter data when the main menu is displayed. Press Esc to return to READY mode.

Column Labels

Column labels are arranged across your spreadsheet; to enter each one, type it and then press the right arrow. In the store example, you would follow these steps:

1. From cell A1, move to cell C1 by pressing → twice.

2. Type **October** in cell C1; press → when finished.

3. Type **November** in cell D1; press → when finished.

4. Type **December** in cell E1; press → when finished.

> **The Enter Key**   When entering your data, you can always press Enter after each entry (instead of the directional arrow) if you want the entry accepted immediately. If you use this key, however, the cell pointer does not move to the next cell.

Row Labels

In this sample worksheet, the row labels extend down column A. Typing in row labels works much like typing in the column labels, except you'll use the down arrow between cell entries. For the store example, follow these steps:

1. From cell A1, move to cell A3 by pressing ↓ twice.

> **Save Time**   Here are two ways to save time and move around the worksheet quickly. Press the **Home** key to return to cell A1. Or, move to any cell location using the GoTo key. Simply press **F5** (GoTo), type in a cell location, and press **Enter**.

2. Type **Cards** in A3 and press ↓.

3. Type **Pens** in A4 and press ↓.

4. Type **Stamps** in A5 and press ↓.

5. Type **Seals** in A6 and press ↓.

Wide Labels   If your labels are too wide to fit into a cell, see Lesson 13 for instructions on changing column widths.

Typing Values

You use the same approach to enter values that you do to enter labels: type the value, and then move to another cell by using an arrow key (the value is then accepted). In the store example, you would follow these steps:

1. Position the cell pointer in cell C3.

2. Type **12** in C3 and press →.

3. Type **10** in D3 and press →.

4. Type **15** in E3 and press ↓.

5. Press ← twice to move the cell pointer back to cell C4.

6. Type **10** in C4 and press →.

7. Type **12** in D4 and press →.

8. Type **15** in E4 and press ↓.

9. Press ← twice to move the cell pointer back to cell C5.

Continue with these same steps to complete the data entry. If you're following the store example, your spreadsheet now looks like Figure 6.2.

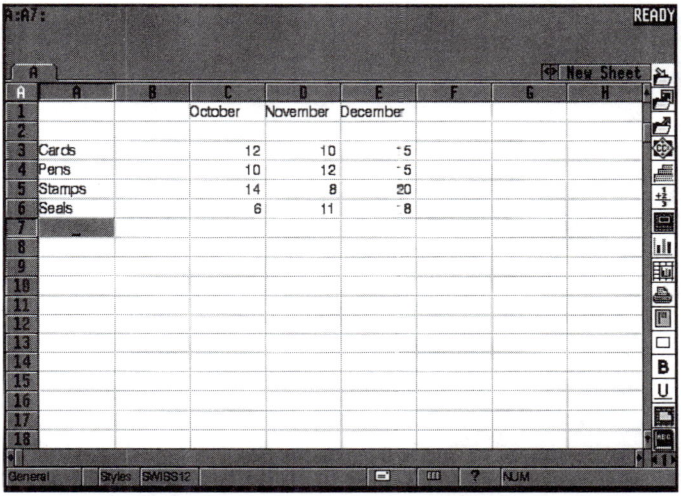

Figure 6.2 The completed sample worksheet.

In this lesson, you learned how to enter labels and values to build a simple spreadsheet. In the next lesson, you will learn how to use ranges for selecting, copying, naming, and deleting columns, rows, and blocks of numbers. You will also learn how to use the pointer-movement keys.

Lesson

Using Ranges

7

In this lesson, you will learn how to select, copy, name, and delete cell ranges.

Range Basics

Sometimes when you are creating or modifying spreadsheets, you will need to work with selected groups of cells (ranges), rather than one individual cell or a whole worksheet. By selecting a range, you can easily copy, format, delete, total, and move that range—whether it's made up of columns, rows, or blocks of labels or numbers.

No Buffalo Here!   A *range* is any highlighted area of cells you may choose. It can be as small as one cell, or as large as the entire worksheet. For instance, you may need to format certain rows or columns of numbers to display dollars and cents. When you select that range, you can format all the cells at once.

Selecting or Highlighting Ranges

Before you copy, move, or name a range of cells, you have to select the range. Only then will 1-2-3 know which cells you want to perform the operation on.

You can select a range by typing in beginning and ending cell addresses, or by highlighting the range with the cell pointer or directional arrows. With the mouse, you can highlight the range by clicking and dragging the mouse.

You can also select a range by entering a range name that you've previously assigned.

Selecting with Cell Addresses

The Copy command provides a good way to learn how to select a range by typing in a cell address at 1-2-3's prompt. To type a cell address, follow these steps:

1. Put the cell pointer in the cell that you want to begin the range you're copying.

2. Select /Copy. 1-2-3 asks which cell to copy from: **Copy FROM**: appears in the control panel (see Figure 7.1).

What's /COPY? Remember, when you see a command in this book that begins with a /, it means to press the / key first to open the main menu, and then select the command from the menu.

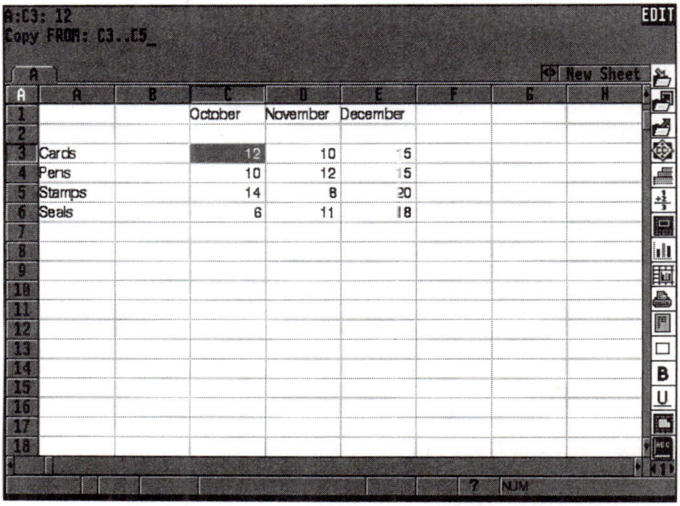

Figure 7.1 The Copy FROM: prompt is displayed in the control panel.

3. Type the cell address from which the range is to start. For instance, if the range starts in C3, type C3.

4. Enter two periods with no spaces (..).

5. Type the cell address at which the range is to end. (If you're following the stationery store example, it ends in C6; the whole range would be C3..C6.)

6. Press Enter.

You will be asked to give another range, showing just where you want to copy TO, but we're only practicing at this point. Stop the copy procedure by pressing Esc. Keep pressing Esc until the **READY** mode appears.

Selecting by Pointing

Here's how to use the keyboard to point to a range and select it:

1. Move the cell pointer onto the cell where the range begins.

2. Select /Copy.

3. When you see the **Copy FROM:** prompt, press ↓ until you've highlighted all the cells to be copied.

4. Press Enter.

You will be asked to give another range, showing just where you want to copy TO, but we're only practicing at this point. Stop the copy procedure by pressing Esc. Keep pressing Esc until the **READY** mode appears.

To use your mouse to point and select, follow these steps:

1. Move the cell pointer onto the cell where the range begins.

2. Move the mouse pointer into the control panel to make the main menu visible.

3. Click on Copy.

4. When you see the **Copy FROM:** prompt, point to the starting cell to be copied.

5. Press and hold the left mouse button. Drag the mouse until all the cells you want to select are highlighted.

6. When the range is highlighted, release the mouse button.

> **Release Me!** Don't worry. You can deselect ranges easily by pressing Esc. Or you can move the mouse pointer away from the selected range and click.

Copying Ranges

You've probably figured out for yourself how to copy a range. After you've answered the **FROM:** prompt, indicating where the range starts and ends, answer the **TO:** prompt, indicating where the data is to be copied. Then press Enter. Figure 7.2 shows a response to the **TO:** prompt.

Erasing a Range

To delete or erase a range, follow these steps:

1. Choose /Range.

2. Select Erase from the Range menu.

3. Select the range or type the range name.

4. Press Enter.

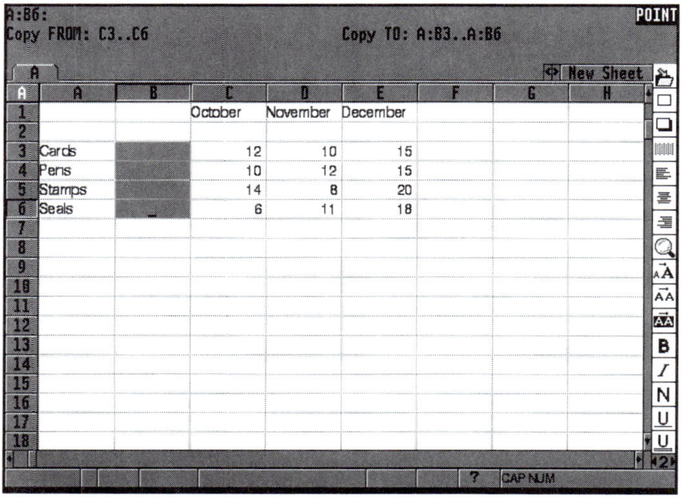

```
A:B6:                                                    POINT
Copy FROM: C3..C6              Copy TO: A:B3..A:B6
```

Figure 7.2   Responding to the TO: prompt.

Naming Ranges of Cells

You can save time by *naming* a range of cells you use often, and then calling up the range name to move data into strategic places. Here's how to name a range:

1. Press / to call up the main menu.

2. Select Range from the main menu.

3. Select Name.

4. Select Create.

5. When 1-2-3 prompts you to **Enter name:**, type in a range name and press Enter. (In the sample worksheet, you could enter the name **items** for the range holding the sales items.)

6. Type in or select the addresses that make up the range you are naming (for this example, choose cells A3..A6).

7. Press Enter, and 1-2-3 assigns the range name to the cell range you've indicated.

Using Named Ranges in a Worksheet

To use the range name when specifying a range, follow these steps:

1. Press / to call up the main menu.

2. Select Copy.

3. Type the range name you assigned (for our example, type items).

4. Press Enter. 1-2-3 accepts the new range, and asks where you want the copy to go.

5. Answer the **TO:** prompt and press Enter.

6. If you are finished copying, press Esc until the **READY** mode appears.

Displaying a List of Range Names

Sometimes it's faster to choose a range name from a list. To get 1-2-3 to display a list of range names, follow these steps:

1. When prompted for a range (for example, in the Copy procedure), press F3. A list of range names appears.

2. Use ← or → to highlight the range name on the list.

3. Press Enter to select the range name.

Deleting a Range Name

To delete a range name, follow these steps:

1. Press / to access the main menu.

2. Choose Range from the main menu.

3. Select Name.

4. Select Delete. A list of range names appears.

5. Highlight the name you want to delete from the list.

6. Press Enter. 1-2-3 deletes the range name, and returns to READY mode.

In this lesson, you learned how to use the Range command to select and copy ranges of data. You also learned how to name ranges and remove range names from the list. In the next lesson, you will discover how to save your worksheet.

Lesson

8

Saving Your Data on a Worksheet

In this lesson, you will learn how to save your data in a 1-2-3 worksheet.

Save What?

When using any software, it's best to learn—and learn quickly—how to save your work. If you don't save your work, all your efforts disappear when you clear the workspace, get a new file, or exit the program (or if there's a power outage).

Saving is a simple process in Lotus 1-2-3. The basic command is /File Save, which copies your worksheet to your hard drive or diskette. Then it's permanently yours.

Some Rules

When saving, you're going to be asked to give your worksheet a name. Here are some naming guidelines:

- Your file name can have up to eight characters. (Remember: 1-2-3 adds an extension of .WK3 automatically.)

- Your file name can be composed of letters, numbers, and the underscore (_) or hyphen (-) characters, or a combination of these.

- Don't use any blank spaces. You may never see your worksheet again if you do!

- Don't use these characters: / \ = + ; : | ! ? * < > "

Just stick with the facts (as the guy from "Dragnet" says). In 1-2-3, stick with eight characters, numbers, the underscore, and hyphen. You'll save yourself from a great big headache!

Saving a Lotus 1-2-3 Worksheet

Make sure that 1-2-3 is in READY mode, and then follow these steps to save a newly created worksheet:

1. Select /File.

2. Select Save. The second line of the control panel displays the path and a file name for new worksheets (example: **File0001.WK3**).

3. Press Esc. Across line 3 of the control panel is a list of the files saved in 1-2-3 (see Figure 8.1).

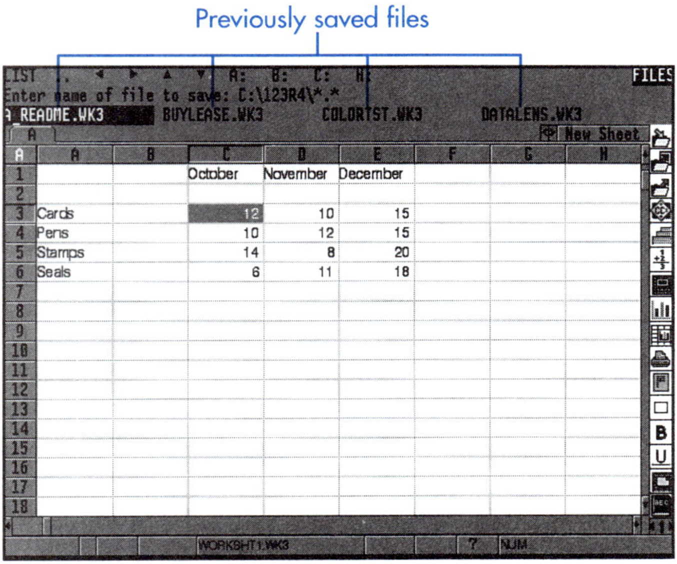

Previously saved files

Figure 8.1   List of files saved in 1-2-3.

4. Press Esc again; the *edit cursor* (a flashing pointer) will take its place at the end of your data's directory name.

5. Type in your file name:

- If the directory showing is the one you want to use to store your file, accept it and type in your file name.

- If you want to use a different directory, use the Backspace key to wipe out the name of the default directory, type in the one you want to use, and then enter your file name.

6. Press Enter, and 1-2-3 saves your worksheet.

Practice Makes Perfect   You should practice saving the stationery store worksheet. Name it something like **Retail**.

Saving and Replacing

You can change a file saved previously in one of two ways:

- Give the worksheet a new name (this way you have copies of both the old and new versions). The steps for saving a worksheet with a new name are the same as those for saving a whole new worksheet.

- Do a *save and replace* to overwrite the original worksheet with the latest version.

To save and replace a 1-2-3 worksheet so it keeps its original file name, follow these steps:

1. Choose /File.

2. Select Save. The existing file name is shown in the control panel.

3. Press Enter. 1-2-3 will prompt you to Cancel, Replace, or BackUp.

4. Highlight one of these options:

Cancel will leave the existing file just as it is, and return you to READY mode.

Replace will overwrite the existing file on your disk, saving the modified version.

BackUp will save the old version of the file under a .BAK extension.

5. Once you've chosen an option, press Enter to save your worksheet.

Quick Save   Use the Save SmartIcon from any palette to save a new or modified worksheet quickly.

Automatically Backing Up Your Files

It's a good idea to have 1-2-3 automatically back up your files. This way, when you get so involved in a worksheet that you forget to save it periodically, you don't have anything to fear: auto backup is there! You can specify how often (in minutes) 1-2-3 backs up your file. Usually, every ten to 20 minutes is a practical choice.

To have 1-2-3 make backups of your files automatically:

1. Choose the /Worksheet Global command. The Global Settings dialog box appears.

2. Click anywhere on the Global Settings dialog box. New buttons appear at the bottom of the dialog box, including the Default Settings button.

3. Click on the Default Settings button. The Default Settings dialog box appears, as shown in Figure 8.2.

4. In the Auto-backup every [ ] minutes box, type an amount. (For example, type 15 to have 1-2-3 back up automatically every 15 minutes.)

Enter a time increment
for automatic backups.

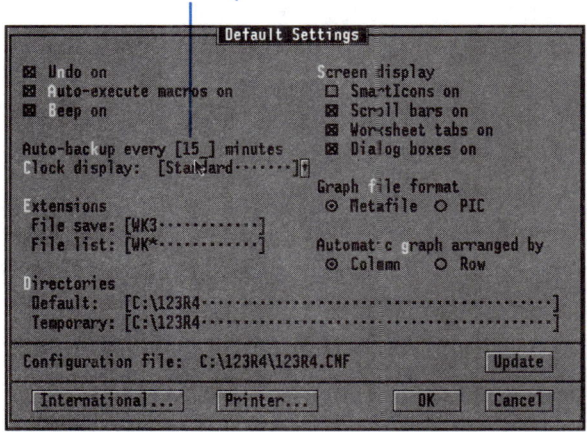

Figure 8.2 Have 1-2-3 automatically back up your files.

5. Click on the Update button.

6. Click on OK.

   In this lesson, you learned how to name and save a new worksheet, how to save and replace a modified worksheet, and how to have 1-2-3 perform automatic backups. In the next lesson, you will have an opportunity to retrieve your worksheet, display a list of files, and undo the Retrieve command.

Lesson

Retrieving a Lotus 1-2-3 Worksheet

In this lesson, you will learn how to retrieve a worksheet saved previously, and how to retrieve Email.

Getting Your Files Back

The longer you work with 1-2-3, the more of a "history" of documents you build up. Fortunately, 1-2-3 makes it easy to bring back (or *retrieve*) worksheets you've created and saved in the past.

Save First Before you retrieve a different file, *be sure to save any current work.* Otherwise, the retrieval process may erase what you have on-screen.

Here are the steps you'll take to bring back an existing worksheet:

1. Choose /File.

2. Select Retrieve. The names of worksheet files saved in the current directory appear across the third line of the control panel. 1-2-3 lists the files alphabetically, as shown in Figure 9.1.

List indicator

```
LIST   ..  ◄  ►  ▲  ▼  A:  B:  C:  H:                              FILES
Enter name of file to retrieve: C:\123R4\*.*
A_README.WK3        BUYLEASE.WK3        COLORTST.WK3      DATALENS.WK3
  A                                                          ⇩ New Sheet
A       A        B        C         D         E       F        G        H
1                        October   November December
2
3   Cards                   12        10        15
4   Pens                    10        12        15
5   Stamps                  14         8        20
6   Seals                    6        11        18
7
8
9
10
11
12
13
14
15
16
17
18
                       WORKSHT1.WK3                       ?    NUM
```

Figure 9.1 Saved worksheet files.

3. Use the arrow keys to scroll through the file names, and highlight (or click on with the mouse) the file name of the worksheet you are retrieving. (If you know the file name, press Esc and enter the name of the file you want to retrieve.)

4. Press Enter. The retrieval is complete.

Full-Screen File List

If scrolling through the control panel's list of files seems too slow, you may find it's quicker to display a full-screen listing.

The fastest way to bring up this list is by clicking on the Retrieve SmartIcon found on palette 1.

Another way to bring up the full-screen file list is to press F3 , or click the mouse on the List indicator in the top left corner of your screen (see Figure 9.1). In both cases, your spreadsheet will disappear, and a list of the files in the current directory will fill the screen, as shown in Figure 9.2.

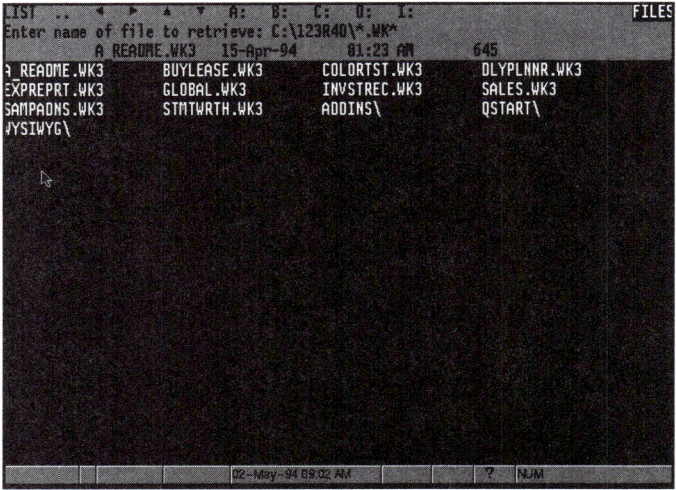

Figure 9.2   Directory contents, as shown by the List feature.

To select the file you want to retrieve from the list:

• Click on its file name.

• Use the arrow keys to move to the file name you want. When it's highlighted, press Enter .

Undoing a Retrieve

If you have one worksheet open and decide you need to look at another one, you're going to simply retrieve the second worksheet, right? Wrong. If you do, you could lose all the data in the first worksheet.

Unfortunately, we all make mistakes; but 1-2-3's creators were kind enough to build in a "back door," in case you forget to save your work before starting the Retrieve process. In fact, if you haven't made any changes to the retrieved file, you can return to your previous worksheet and save it.

If you find yourself in this situation, press Alt+F4 to undo the Retrieve. The previous worksheet appears on-screen. Save your changes and retrieve your file again.

Next Time!   If the Undo feature isn't turned on, you won't be able to save the file that's been deleted. But you can protect yourself should this ever happen again. Turn on the Undo feature by selecting the Undo option in the Default Settings dialog box (accessed by the /Worksheet Global Default Settings command sequence).

You can undo quickly by using the Undo SmartIcon found in palette 5.

Opening Multiple Files

You can have more than one file open at a time if you wish. Instead of using the File Retrieve command, you'll use the File Open command. You can open as many files as your computer's memory supports.

To open multiple files:

1. Position the mouse pointer in the control panel or press / to display the main menu.

2. Choose /File.

3. Select *Open*. 1-2-3 asks you if you want the new file to appear before the current worksheet or after.

4. To work on the new file immediately, choose *Before*. To place the new file behind the current worksheet, choose *After*.

5. Use the arrow keys to scroll through the file names, and highlight (or click on with the mouse) the filename of the worksheet you want to open.

6. Press *Enter*. The file appears on-screen. 1-2-3 places a tab at the top of each worksheet file so you can keep track of the files and switch to them easily (see Figure 9.3).

7. Repeat steps 1 through 6 to open additional files.

Click on a tab to switch
to a different file.

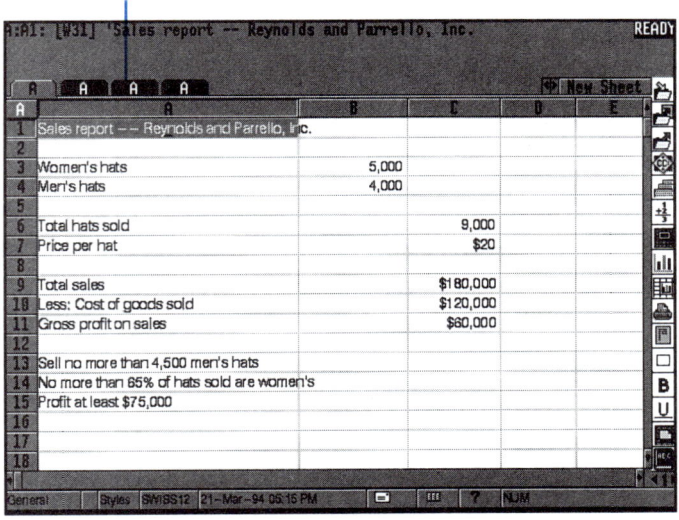

Figure 9.3 Opening multiple files in 1-2-3.

Previewing Files   If you don't remember the name of the file you want to open, use the /File View command to view the contents of your files before opening them.

Retrieving Email

If you work on a network and use cc:Mail Release 4.02 for DOS, you're sure to appreciate 1-2-3 Release 4's new feature that enables you to retrieve Email without having to interrupt your 1-2-3 session. What's more, retrieving Email is as simple as clicking on an icon.

Retrieving Mail   To retrieve incoming Email, simply click on the Retrieve Email icon on the status bar. 1-2-3 displays the Email message on the screen.

Sending Email   You can also send Email without having to quit 1-2-3. Click on the cc:Mail SmartIcon on palette 1, or choose the /Tools Email command. You can send a text message, range, or file.

In this lesson, you learned how to retrieve a worksheet file and an Email message. In the next lesson, you will learn how to create formulas and use functions.

Lesson

Working with Formulas and Functions

In this lesson, you will learn how to build, enter, and edit formulas, and use functions in worksheets.

Spreadsheet Power

You can place a lot of letters and numbers into spreadsheet cells. You can enter numbers in various formats—including fractions, decimals, and dates. You can put in letters (as labels) that describe the contents of particular rows or columns.

Here's something else you can put into your worksheet's cells, something that gives your 1-2-3 worksheet real oomph and power: formulas.

Calculatin' A *formula* performs calculations based on the numbers in other cells—but it will only get the right answer if you build it according to a specific order of operations (see "Order of Precedence," later in this lesson).

You can build your own worksheet-unique formulas—and many 1-2-3 users are very sophisticated at building formulas. You can also use some built-in formulas called *@functions* (pronounced "at-functions").

Formulas are really what make your spreadsheet worth the time and effort. You can use them to:

- Add up a group of numbers.

- Find and display the average of a range of numbers.

- Analyze the values in groups of cells statistically.

- Perform a "what-if" analysis, using different numbers to explore different possibilities.

Building Your Own Formulas

Suppose you want to add values you have entered in cells C3 through C6, placing the total in cell C7. Follow these steps:

1. Retrieve your worksheet (see Lesson 8 for instructions).

2. Move the cell pointer to cell C7.

3. Press + on the number pad. All 1-2-3 formulas must begin with a number or one of these characters: + - @ .

4. Type C3+C4+C5+C6.

5. Press Enter.

The result appears in cell C7. Look at the first line of the control panel (shown in Figure 10.1) to see your formula.

Formula Operators

Formulas are often somewhat lengthy, and they do all sorts of things—like add, subtract, multiply, divide, and more. Mathematical symbols, called *operators*, tell 1-2-3 how to treat the values that appear in your formula. Table 10.1 shows the operators you can use.

Formula ─── Result of formula

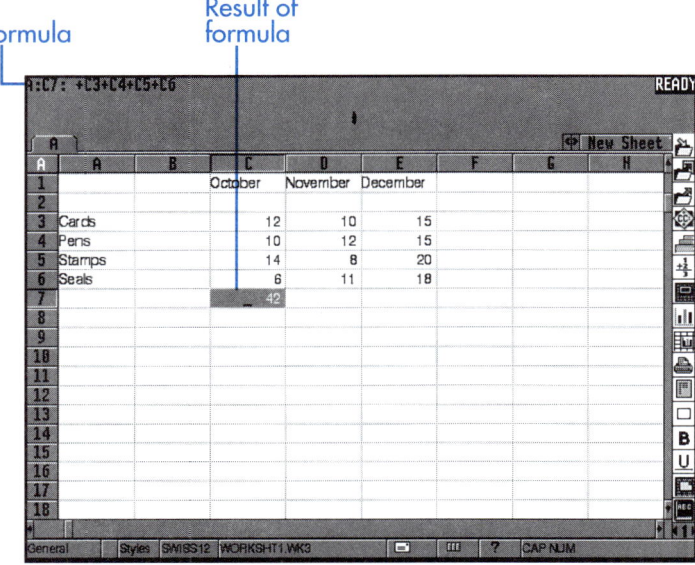

Figure 10.1 A formula is displayed in line 1 of the control panel.

Table 10.1 1-2-3's Formula Operators

Operator	Description
+	Add
–	Subtract
*	Multiply
/	Divide
^	Treat as exponent
>	Is greater than
<	Is less than
>=	Is greater than or equal to
<=	Is less than or equal to
<>	Is not equal to

To enter a series of values in cells A1, B1, and C1, and enter a formula in D1 determining the average of these values, you would enter the formula **(A1+B1+C1)/3** in cell D1. This tells 1-2-3 to add the values in cells A1, B1, and C1 and then divide the total by 3. The result is then inserted in cell D1.

Order of Precedence

Spreadsheet programs perform operations in a formula in a particular order; some operators (such as multiplication) have power over others (such as addition). In other words, when 1-2-3 sees a formula that contains several operators (for example, addition and multiplication), it adheres to rules about which operator is processed first—regardless of their physical location in the formula. 1-2-3 performs operations according to the following *order of precedence*:

- First: exponential equations

- Second: multiplication and division

- Third: addition and subtraction

Parentheses can be used to control the order of operations, however. For example, in the averaging formula, if you leave out the parentheses, you'll get the wrong answer! The value in C1 will be divided by 3, and that result will be added to A1+B1 (because of the order of precedence). To determine the total of A1 through C1 first, you need to enclose that group of values in parentheses.

Wrong Answer   If your formula doesn't work or you get an error, make sure there is a closing parenthesis to accompany each opening parenthesis. Then check the order of operations. Here's a tip to help you remember the order of precedence: "**M**y **D**ear **A**unt **S**ally!" (multiply, divide, add, subtract).

Editing Formulas

If you must edit your formula, and prefer not to type it in again, follow these steps:

1. Move your cell pointer to the cell that displays the formula you intend to edit.

2. Press F2 (the Edit key). This puts 1-2-3 in EDIT mode.

3. Make your changes. (Use Backspace to delete characters you don't want; use the left arrow key to move back without deleting characters.)

4. Press Enter. After making your changes, 1-2-3 puts you back in READY mode.

> **Check Your Formulas** If you have a complicated worksheet with many formulas, sometimes you may need to display all of them. Choose /Worksheet and Select Global Format. Then choose Text. The formulas will appear in their appropriate on-screen locations. Return to normal display by selecting /Worksheet Global Format General.

1-2-3's Functions

You'll find that 1-2-3 comes with a set of useful preset functions. (These must begin with an @ sign. A table of 1-2-3 functions is included in the back of this book.)

You can, for instance, total the column of values in cells C3 through C6 by typing @sum(C3..C6) in cell A11. To assign this function, follow these steps:

1. Using the arrow keys, place the cell pointer in cell A11.

2. Type **@SUM(**.

3. Enter the range of cells to total by typing in the addresses, pointing to the range, or using a range name.

4. Type the closing parenthesis **)**. The result in our example should read **@SUM(C3..C6)**.

5. Press Enter. The result is placed in cell A11.

Sum It Up   To total a range of cells quickly, move the cursor below the last value in a column or to the right of the last value in a row of numbers. Then select the Sum SmartIcon from palette 1. 1-2-3 places the total value of the cells in the cell in which the cursor is located.

In this lesson, you learned how to create and edit formulas. You also learned that 1-2-3 has a set of built-in formulas that are easy to use. In the next lesson, you will learn how to use three add-in programs that enable you to check formulas, change them, and analyze data in a worksheet file to solve what-if problems.

Lesson

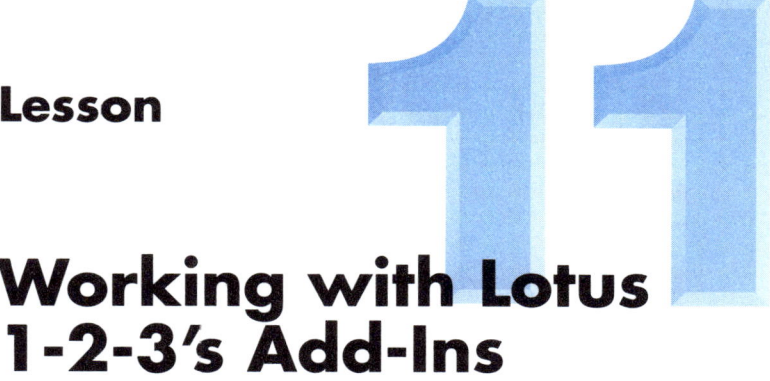

Working with Lotus 1-2-3's Add-Ins

In this lesson, you will learn how to use three special add-in programs—Auditor, Backsolver, and Solver.

Attaching an Add-In

Before using an add-in program, you must load it into memory. Certain add-ins, such as Wysiwyg and Viewer, are automatically loaded when you start 1-2-3. To load the others, follow these steps (alternatively, you can use the /Tools Config Addin command).

What's an Add-In? An *add-in* is a special program (like Wysiwyg or Auditor) created by Lotus or another software developer that you can use with 1-2-3 to enhance its capabilities.

1. Press Alt+F10. A menu appears.

2. Choose Load, and then select the add-in. (For our example, select Auditor.)

3. Choose a key combination that will activate the add-in. (For our example, pick Alt+F7.) Then click on 1, or move the cursor to it and press the Enter key.

4. Press Esc to return to your worksheet.

Once the add-in has been attached, you can invoke it at any time during the 1-2-3 session by pressing the function key to which it is attached (in this example, Alt+F7).

Auditor

If you have an enormous worksheet containing many formulas, it can be time-consuming to analyze the structure of the worksheet, locate formulas, and find the sources of errors. 1-2-3 provides an add-in program, Auditor, that can help you do the following things:

- Track formulas and their relationships.

- Locate possible circular references.

- Ensure that certain formulas are calculating in the correct order of precedence.

When you activate Auditor (using its key combination), a menu appears, as shown in Figure 11.1. These settings display the current audit range and audit mode. The default audit range includes all worksheets in all files in memory, and the default audit mode is Highlight.

Where's My Dictionary? An *audit range* is a range that Auditor is analyzing. The *audit mode* determines what type of function Auditor will perform (Highlight, List, or Trace).

Table 11.1 shows Auditor's commands and the tasks they perform when you activate them.

Table 11.1 Auditor's Commands

Command	Task
Circs	Shows the cells making up a circular reference.

continues

Table 11.1 Continued

Command	Task
Dependents	Shows which formulas in the audit range refer to one specific cell.
Formulas	Shows which formulas make up the audit range.
Options	Lets you change audit range and audit mode.
Precedents	Shows which cells in the audit range are data sources for a specific formula.
Quit	Returns you to 1-2-3's READY mode.
Recalc-List	Shows all recalculated formulas, in order.

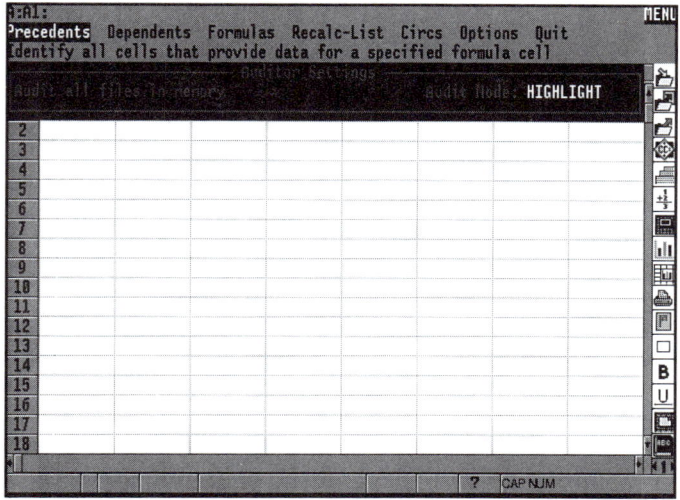

Figure 11.1 Using the Auditor.

Circs

To give you an idea of how to use Auditor, let's look at the Circs option.

A *circular reference* occurs when a formula refers (directly or indirectly) to itself. For instance, if cell A7 contains the formula @AVG(A7..A15), the circular reference is *direct* (A7 is in the formula). If cell A1 contains +A2, cell A2 contains +A3, and cell A3 contains +A1, the circular reference is *indirect* (you loop back to the starting point, cell A1). Both direct and indirect circular references cause 1-2-3 to display the **CIRC** indicator near the bottom of your screen (see Figure 11.2).

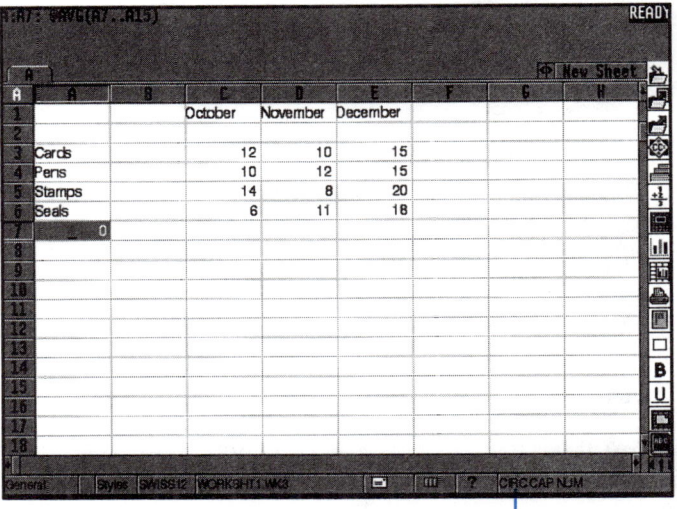

L— CIRC indicator

Figure 11.2 A circular reference in a 1-2-3 worksheet.

Although the **CIRC** indicator warns you that you've created a circular reference, it doesn't help you determine *where* that reference might be. That's why you need the

Auditor program itself. Here's an example of how to use Auditor to identify the circular reference.

1. Invoke Auditor (press Alt+F7 or whatever key combination you defined).

2. Select Circs from the Auditor menu. Auditor displays the cells involved in a circular reference.

3. Press Esc three times to return to your worksheet and the READY mode.

Detaching an Add-In

The more add-ins you attach, the more memory 1-2-3 requires. Therefore, you should detach any add-ins you are not using. To detach Auditor—or any other add-in—follow these steps:

1. Press Alt+F10.

2. Choose Remove from the menu, and press Enter.

3. Select Auditor (or the appropriate add-in).

4. Press Esc.

Backsolver

Perhaps you have a specific target to achieve for retail sales profit margin, and you want to see what total sales must be reached to attain that target. Backsolver is an add-in that lets you calculate a formula to achieve a value (your target profit margin, for example) by changing one or more variables that affect the results of the formula.

Using Backsolver is like playing Jeopardy: you provide the answer, and Backsolver provides the question (the variables). If you change one of the variables, Backsolver will tell you how the change affects the other variables, assuming the answer remains the same.

Caution: Save Those Original Values When you use Backsolver, 1-2-3 replaces the original values in the variable cells with Backsolver's answers. If you don't want to lose your original values, either save your file before using Backsolver, or make a copy of the original values in another location.

First, you must attach the Backsolver add-in. (Follow the steps earlier in this lesson.) Then, with the appropriate worksheet open, follow these steps:

1. In a cell (which becomes the *formula cell*) or range, type in the formula you want Backsolver to use.

2. Decide on the result you want to reach and the variables you will change to reach it.

3. Press Alt+F10, select Invoke, and select Backsolver.

4. When the Backsolver menu appears, choose Formula-Cell.

5. Indicate the name of the range (or the address of the formula cell) in which you typed your formula in step 1.

6. Choose Value.

7. Type in the value you want the formula cell's formula to result in. You can enter a formula instead; Backsolver will convert it to a number before solving the problem.

8. Choose Adjustable.

9. Identify (either by address or range name) the cells containing values you will let Backsolver change.

10. Choose Solve.

11. When Backsolver finishes and you have analyzed its answers, choose Quit. READY mode reappears.

Solver

Solver lets you explore different results of your formula by running different combinations of values through it—a process called *what-if analysis*. If you want to improve the profitability of your business, for instance, use Solver to experiment with different combinations of sales quotas and cost cuts.

Before using this add-in, first enter *logical formulas* into your worksheet; these tell Solver the conditions you want it to meet while calculating your answer. If you want an interest rate below 13 percent, for example, you can specify it with a logical formula such as +LOAN<=.13.

Solver then uses the cells you specify (as well as other information in the worksheet) to help you analyze and solve problems. Using Solver is complicated, beyond the scope of this book, but you can find help for it in Chapter 17 of 1-2-3's Reference.

This lesson previewed three of 1-2-3's powerful add-ins, Auditor, Backsolver, and Solver. The next lesson moves into copying and moving cells, with special emphasis on absolute and relative cell references.

Lesson

12

Copying and Moving Cells

In this lesson, you'll learn to move and copy the contents of your 1-2-3 worksheet cells.

You may have a great formula you'd like to use elsewhere in your worksheet. 1-2-3 makes copying and moving the contents of cells a simple task.

In this lesson you'll begin with the basics of copying and moving, and then move into the more sophisticated topic of using relative and absolute cell references. You'll need to know about cell referencing if you're going to move or copy formulas.

Copying Cell Contents

You can copy the contents of one cell or of many cells (a range of cells). For instance, you may need to copy a range of numbers located in cells A5 through A25 to the location B5 through B25. Here are the steps to take:

1. Select Copy. The **Copy FROM:** prompt appears (see Figure 12.1).

2. Perform one of the following steps:

- If you're copying a single cell, move the cell pointer to that cell or type its address.

- If you're copying a range of cells, select the range of cells to copy by typing the range or by pointing to it.

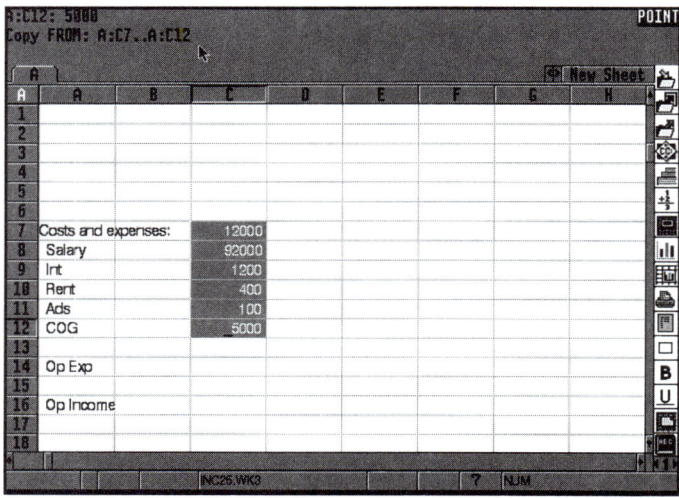

Figure 12.1 The copy FROM: prompt appears when the Copy command is selected.

3. Press Enter. The **Copy TO:** prompt appears.

4. Perform one of the following steps:

- If you are copying one cell to another cell, move the pointer to the destination cell or type its address.

- If you are copying a range of cells to an area of identical size, put the cell pointer on the cell that begins the destination range, or type that cell's address.

- If the destination range has a size or shape different from that of the range being copied, either highlight the destination range or type its complete address.

5. Press Enter. 1-2-3 copies the indicated range of cells, as shown in Figure 12.2.

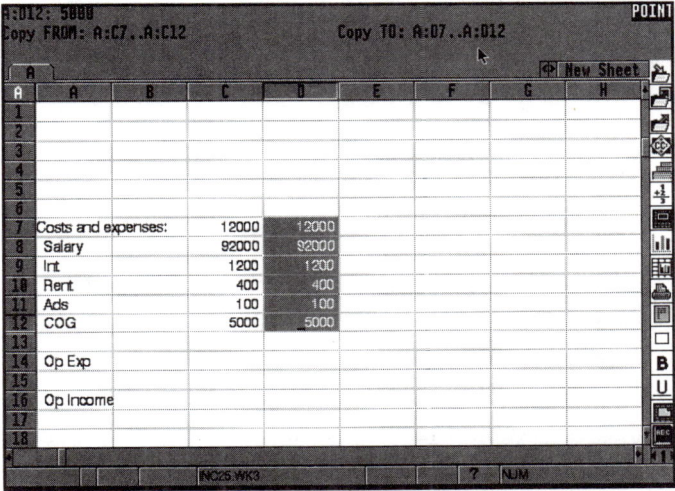

Figure 12.2 1-2-3 copies a range of cells.

If you want to copy a range of cells quickly, select the range, select the Copy Range SmartIcon from palette 5, and choose the destination range.

Moving Cells

Moving cells works almost exactly like copying cells. The difference? You're physically moving the cell's actual contents (rather than a duplicate of those contents) to another location. Follow these steps to move cells:

1. Choose /Move. The **Move FROM:** prompt appears.

2. Perform one of the following steps:

- If you're moving a single cell, click on that cell or type its address.

- If you're moving a range of cells, select the range of cells to move (type the range or select it). For example, to move the cell range referred to in the earlier section, type in **A5..A25**.

3. Press Enter. The **Move TO:** prompt appears.

4. Perform one of the following steps:

- If you are moving one cell to another cell, move the pointer to the destination cell or type its address.

- If you are moving a range of cells to an area that's the same size, position the cell pointer at the beginning cell of the destination range, or type the cell's address. (For our example, you would type **B5..B25**.)

- If the destination range differs in size or shape from the range being moved, either type the complete address of the destination range or highlight it.

5. Press Enter. 1-2-3 removes the cells from their original position and places them in the new location.

Quick Move   You can move a selected range of cells quickly with the Move Range SmartIcon on palette 5. Before you select the icon, be sure to select the range you want to move.

Relative and Absolute References

1-2-3 doesn't just blindly move and copy; it tries to anticipate your needs. For example, let's say you have a formula that adds the contents of a column. When you copy that formula into a different column, you want the formula to report the total for the new column, not the old one.

1-2-3 knows that you probably want to copy the meaning of the formula, not the actual cell references. That's why all cell references in 1-2-3 are *relative* unless you specify otherwise. The formulas work "relative to" their surroundings—when you move or copy a formula, its cell addresses change to reflect its new place in the worksheet.

For instance, you could place a formula in cell A5 to average three numbers in column A (A1..A3). If you copied this formula to B5, 1-2-3 would change your formula automatically to reflect the new cell addresses. The formula +(A1+A2+A3)/3 would become +(B1+B2+B3)/3 when copied to B5.

There are times, however, when you may need to override this relative referencing, to make a cell address *absolute*. For example, you may want the formula in cell A5 to remain +(A1+A2+A3)/3 no matter where you put a copy of it. To create an absolute address to a cell, you must enter a dollar sign ($) before both the column and row of each cell address in the formula. For our example in cell A5, it would look like this: +($A$1+$A$2+$A$3)/3. The control panel in Figure 12.3 shows an example of an absolute cell reference.

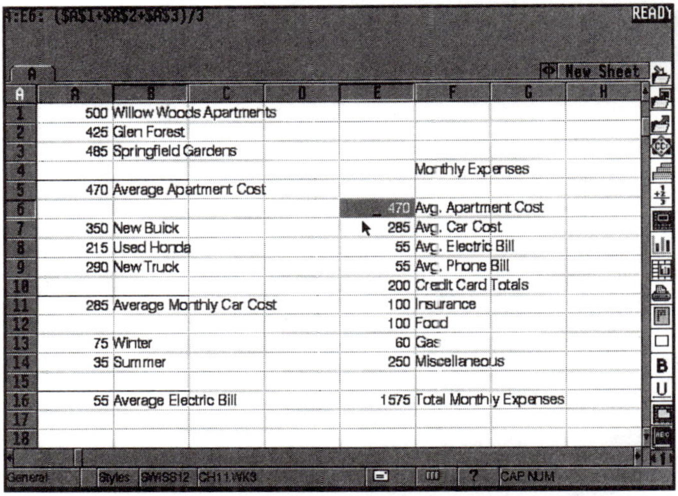

Figure 12.3 A formula indicating absolute cell reference.

This lesson showed you how to copy and move cell contents throughout your worksheet. You also learned how to change relative cell references to absolute. Read Lesson 13 to learn how to edit the contents of cells.

Editing and Deleting Cells

In this lesson, you'll learn how to edit cell contents, delete unneeded cells, recalculate formulas manually, attach a note to a cell, and spell-check your worksheet.

No one's perfect! Sometimes we need to delete a little here or add a little there. 1-2-3 enables you to make such changes—and more—with a minimum of effort.

Cell Editing

To edit a cell, just highlight it, press F2, and then use the editing keys shown in Table 13.1 to make your changes. Here are the exact steps to follow:

1. Move the cell pointer to the cell to be edited.

2. Press F2. The **EDIT** indicator appears (see Figure 13.1).

3. Make your changes, using the keys shown in Table 13.1.

4. Press Enter to record changes and return to the READY mode.

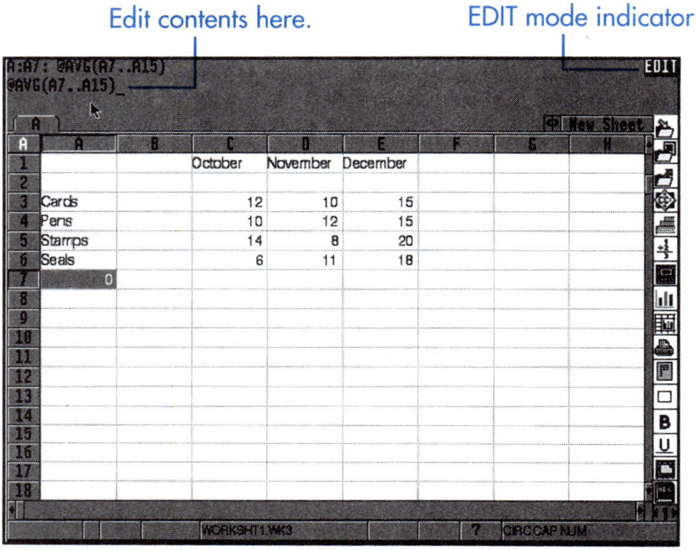

Edit contents here.

EDIT mode indicator

Figure 13.1 The Edit mode is activated.

Table 13.1 Major Editing Keys

Key	Performs
← or →	Moves one character left or right in the edit line.
Backspace	Moves the cursor left, deleting a character.
Del	Deletes the character the cursor highlights.
End	Moves cursor right to the end of the edit line.
Esc	Removes the characters in the edit line.

Key	Performs
Home	Moves cursor left to the start of the edit line.
Ins	Toggles between INSERT and OVERTYPE mode.

Don't Mess Up　Be judicious when making your cell changes. Watch for reversed parentheses, extra quotation marks, and forgotten dollar signs (which indicate absolute cell references).

Deleting Cell Contents

When you delete the contents of a cell, the cell is still there; it's just emptied. Follow these steps to erase the contents of a single cell:

1. Move the cell pointer to the cell you want to erase.

2. Select /Range.

3. Choose Erase.

4. Press Enter. The cell is erased and is replaced with a blank cell.

　　You can erase an entire range of cells at once; the procedure is explained in Lesson 7. To remove entire rows or columns, including the empty cells, see Lesson 14.

Quick Delete　Use the Delete SmartIcon to erase cells and ranges of cells. Highlight the range to be erased and then select the Delete SmartIcon from palette 5.

Recalculating Formulas

1-2-3 calculates formulas automatically when you enter them into your worksheet. Every time you enter numbers into a cell that is referenced in the formula, 1-2-3 recalculates again. If you have a large spreadsheet, waiting for the formulas to recalculate can be annoying.

One solution is to set 1-2-3 for manual recalculation, so you can recalculate whenever you like (and only when you tell it to). The following procedure sets 1-2-3 so that it recalculates whenever you press the F9 key.

1. Select /Worksheet Global. The Global Settings dialog box appears, as shown in Figure 13.2.

2. Press F2 to edit the dialog box.

3. Under Recalculation, click on the Automatic option to unmark its check box.

4. Click on the OK button.

Upon returning to your worksheet, you will have set 1-2-3 to calculate (or recalculate) only when you press F9 (the Calc key). You can change back to automatic recalculation by following steps 1 and 2 again, and choosing Automatic.

Don't Forget!   If you set your spreadsheet for Manual recalculation, you must press F9 to perform the actual calculations. It's critical that you remember to press F9 before quitting and saving the worksheet.

Works the Same   Selecting the Calc SmartIcon from icon palette 6 is just like pressing the F9 (Calc) key: it recalculates formulas. When 1-2-3 is calculating formulas, the **CALC** indicator appears on the status bar.

Unmark this box for manual recalculation.

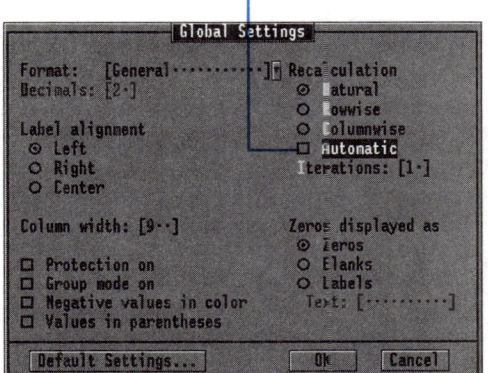

Figure 13.2   Selecting manual recalculation.

Attaching a Note to a Cell

One of Release 4's new features lets you attach notes to
worksheet cells. These notes can serve as helpful reminders
to you, or as extra information or tips for someone else who
will be using the worksheet. You can display the notes full-
size, hide them altogether, or mark them with an icon.

To attach a note to a cell:

1. Move the cell pointer to the cell you want to anno-
tate.

2. Select the Tools command from the main menu.

3. Select the Notepad Add command from the Tools
menu. A notepad appears below the cell (see Figure
13.3).

4. Type the message you want to attach to the cell.

5. Press Esc to save and exit from the note.

To edit, delete, and configure notes, use the commands on the /Tools Notepad menu.

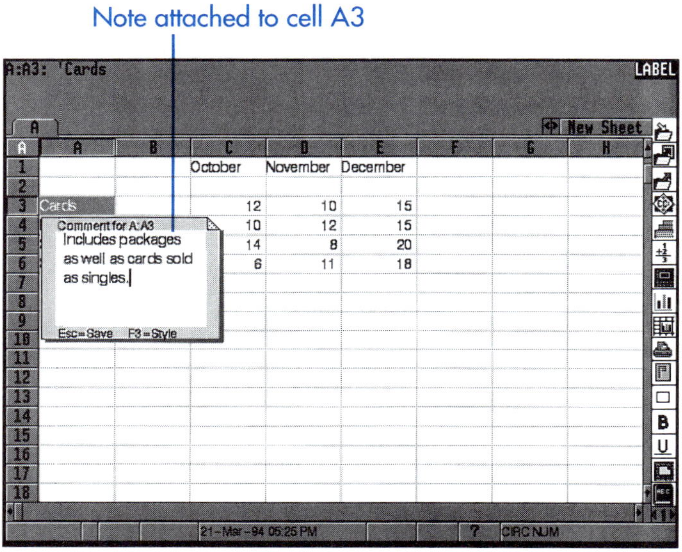

Note attached to cell A3

Figure 13.3 Attaching a note to a cell.

Spell Checking Cell Contents

It's always a smart move to spell check your worksheet, especially if you have a lot of text in it. In addition to mis-spelled words, 1-2-3's spell checker catches repeated words, and checks capitalized words and words with numbers for accuracy. You can spell check an entire file, one worksheet, or a range of cells.

To spell check a range of cells:

1. Select /Tools.

2. Choose Spell. The Spell Check dialog box appears, as shown in Figure 13.4.

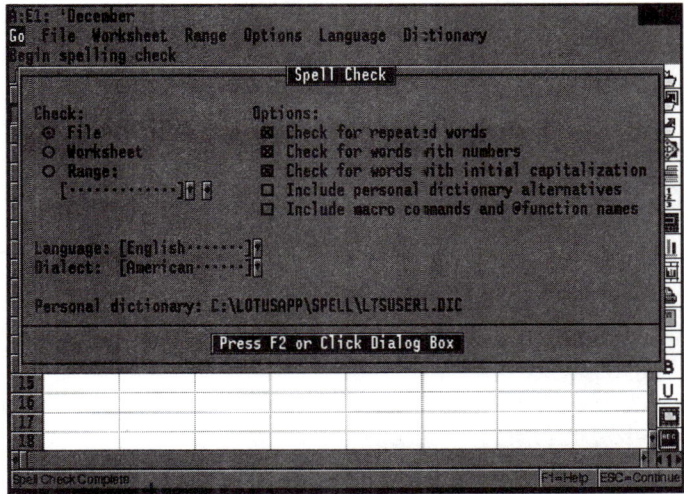

Status line tells you when the
spell check process is
complete.

Figure 13.4 The Spell Check dialog box.

3. Press F2 to edit the dialog box.

4. Under Check, choose Range.

5. Type the range you want to spell check.

6. Select the Go command to start the spell check.
1-2-3 scans the range for spelling errors, and pre-
sents suspected misspelled words to you. You can
either change or ignore these words.

1-2-3 flashes a message on the status bar when it has
finished spell checking the range.

This lesson showed you how to use 1-2-3's powerful
editing capabilities. Next, you'll learn how to format your
worksheet.

14

Changing the Look of a Worksheet

In this lesson, you will learn how to change the cell format and column widths, and how to align labels.

1-2-3 offers you many options for customizing the appearance of your worksheet. You can use these options to make your worksheets look especially distinctive for others to enjoy by following the directions in this lesson, and continuing in Lesson 15.

Changing Cell Format

You have the choice of several different cell *formats* (ways of displaying values and labels in worksheet cells). For instance, you can display some values with one decimal place (25.5) and others with a percent sign (25%).

You can quickly change the format of a cell or range by using the Format pick list on the status bar. Just highlight the range, click the Format button on the status bar (see Figure 14.1), and click on the new format.

Additionally, you can change the cell format in a range with /Range Format. To change cells to display currency, for instance, follow these steps.

1. Move the cell pointer to a cell, or select a range of cells.

2. Select /Range.

3. For this example, select Format and choose Currency.

4. Press Enter. This accepts the default number of 2 decimal places.

5. Press Enter again to complete the format for currency.

Table 14.1 lists the major numeric formatting options, and their effects on the way values are displayed.

Table 14.1 Major Numeric Formats

Format	Affects the Displayed Values This Way
, (comma)	Commas separate thousands; 15 or fewer decimal places; minus sign or parentheses to show negative numbers; a leading zero for decimal places. Example: 987344 can become 987,344.
Currency	Commas separate thousands; 15 or fewer decimal places; minus sign or parentheses indicate negative numbers; currency symbols included. Example: 2345.0 can become $2,345.00.
Fixed	15 or fewer decimal places; minus sign indicates negative numbers; decimal values have a leading zero. Example: 23.89 can become 24.
General	Minus sign indicates negative numbers; no commas separate thousands; no trailing zeros. Example: 134,00.20 becomes 13400.2.

continues

Table 14.1 Continued

Format	Affects the Displayed Values This Way
Percent	Percentages with 15 or fewer decimal places. Example: .089 becomes 8.9%.
Scientific	Shows values in scientific notation; 15 or fewer decimal places; exponent from −99 through +99. Example: −22 becomes −2.20E+01.
Text	Formulas shown as entered (not as calculated values). Example: +A3+B3 would be displayed instead of the numerical sum of the cells A3 and B3.

Use the SmartIcons from palette 6 to format a range of cells for currency, percent, and decimal places.

Changing Column Widths

1-2-3 sets all column widths to 9 characters, by default. Often this width isn't sufficient to display numbers that you've formatted as currency with 2 decimal places. When a cell isn't wide enough to display all of a number, you will see asterisks instead, as in Figure 14.1.

To widen all the columns in a worksheet, follow these instructions:

1. Select /Worksheet.

2. Choose Global (which affects the entire worksheet). The Global Settings dialog box appears, as shown in Figure 14.2.

3. Press F2 or click on the dialog box to edit it.

4. Next to Column width, type a new number (from 1 to 240) and click OK.

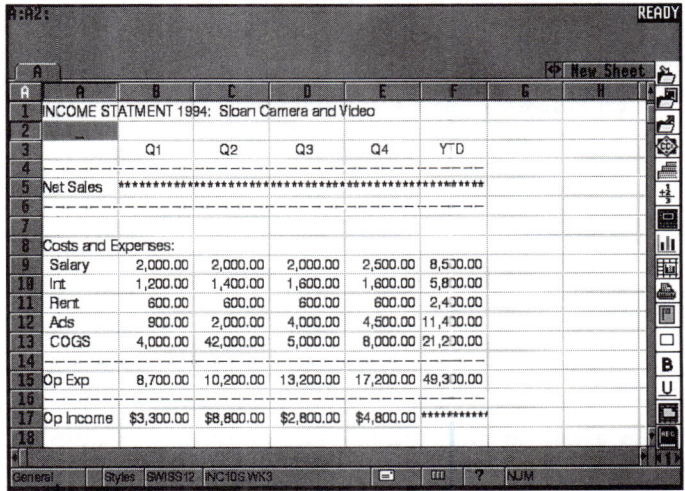

Click here to display
Format pick list.

Number is too
wide in this cell.

Figure 14.1   Asterisks replace a lengthy number until columns are reformatted to hold the wide number.

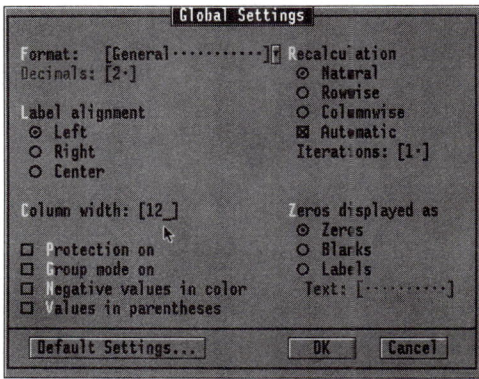

Figure 14.2   Selecting Column Width to widen a column.

Single Column Width, Quick Change
You can also change the width of a single
column. Put the cursor in the column you want to
change, and use the /Worksheet Column Set-width
series of commands.

The Widest Cell   You can instantly size an
entire column to fit the widest cell in that column
by choosing the /Range Column Fit-Widest
command.

Aligning Labels

Column labels typically don't line up with the figures in the
columns until they are realigned by inserting a *label prefix*.
By default, labels are left-aligned, and columns of values are
right-aligned. Table 14.2 shows 1-2-3's label prefixes, and
how they affect label alignment.

Table 14.2   1-2-3 Label Prefixes

Prefix	Cell Display	Alignment
'	label	left
^	label	centered
"	label	right
\	labellabellabel	repeating

To change the default of a left-aligned label, type in the
alternative label prefix when entering the label (see Figure
14.3). You can also change the alignment of a label (or range
of labels) by following these steps.

Label prefix   Centered label

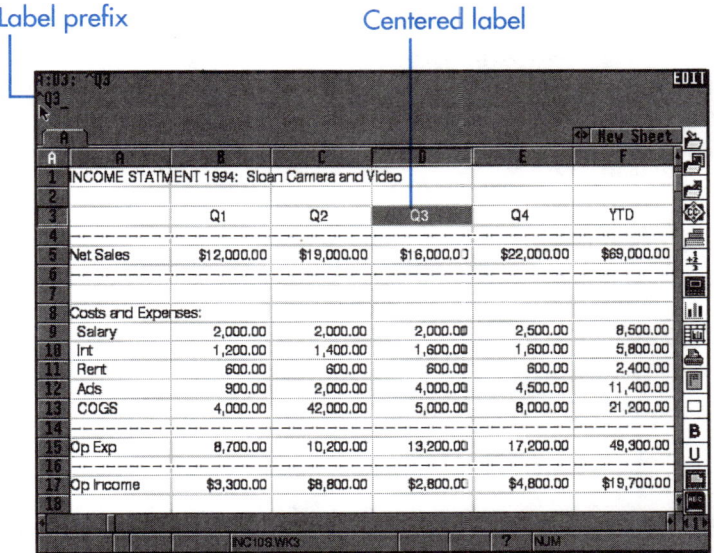

Figure 14.3 Label prefix for centered labels.

1. Choose /Range.

3. Choose Label.

4. Choose an alignment (Left, Right, or Center).

5. Type a cell or range of cells.

6. Press Enter.

To change the formatting of a label quickly, use these SmartIcons from palette 2: Left, Right, or Center.

To add emphasis in a worksheet, use these SmartIcons from palettes 1 and 2 to add bold, italic, and underline formatting attributes to labels.

In this lesson, you learned how to customize your worksheet by changing the cell format and column widths, and by aligning labels. In the next lesson, you will learn how to insert rows, delete unwanted rows, and use automatic formatting.

15

More Formatting

In this lesson, you will learn how to insert and delete rows and columns, and use automatic formatting techniques.

Inserting Rows and Columns

Special formatting techniques can help you really show off your worksheet. For instance, try inserting several blank rows and columns in your worksheet to set off the data. The added "white space" can give your worksheet an attractive look, in addition to making it easier to read and understand.

In Figure 15.1, notice how extra space (inserted rows) was used to set off column labels. The space was then filled with asterisks.

To insert a row or column, begin by moving the cell pointer to any cell in the row below where you want the new row to appear, or the column to the right of where you want the new column to appear.

1. Select /Worksheet.

2. Select Insert.

3. Choose Row or Column.

4. When you are prompted, enter a range and press Enter.

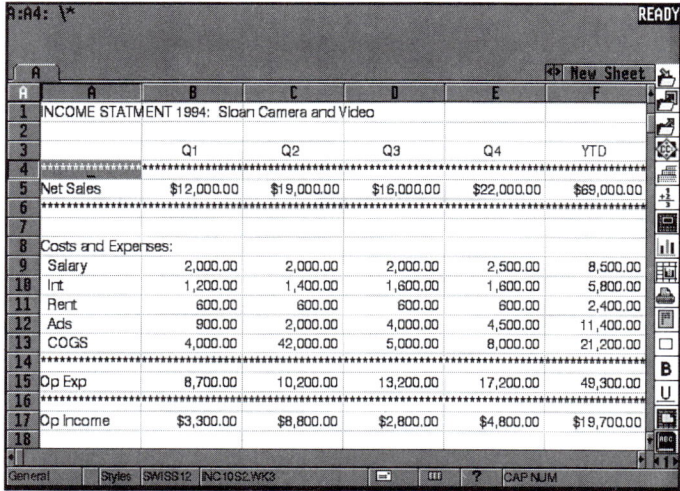

Figure 15.1   Using added space to set off data.

Use these SmartIcons to insert rows or columns into your worksheet. Highlight the row below or the column to the right of where you want to insert the row or column, and select either the Insert Row SmartIcon or the Insert Column SmartIcon from palette 5.

Automatic Formatting

How would you like to enter data and format the cell in the same step? With the Automatic Formatting option, 1-2-3 formats cells according to the way values look when you enter them. If you enter $35.00, for instance, 1-2-3 formats the cell as Currency, 2 decimal places. The following steps show you how to turn this feature on:

1. Select /Worksheet.

2. Choose Global.

3. Select Format.

4. Select Other.

5. Select Automatic.

Any cells that haven't been formatted with the /Range Format command are now set for automatic formatting.

In this lesson, you learned how to insert and delete rows and columns and use automatic formatting techniques. In the next lesson, you will learn how to further enhance your worksheets by using Wysiwyg.

Lesson 16

Enhancing Your Spreadsheet with Wysiwyg

In this lesson, you will learn how to further enhance your worksheet using Wysiwyg.

What's Wysiwyg?

Wysiwyg is an add-in program that lets you see your worksheet on-screen looking similar to how it will be printed. The funny-sounding name (pronounced "wizzy-wig") stands for "what you see is what you get," and what it says is what it means: the feature shows you, on-screen, a close replica of your final printed worksheet.

> **Attach It First**   If the Wysiwyg add-in isn't attached automatically when you start 1-2-3, you will need to attach it. See the first section of Lesson 10 for instructions.

Changing Type (Font) Styles

The quickest way to change fonts is to highlight the range you want to change, click on the Font icon on the status bar (see Figure 16.1), and click on the new style. Another way is to use the Wysiwyg Format menu. Follow these steps to use the Format menu to change the font for a range in the worksheet:

1. Activate the Wysiwyg menu by pressing : (colon).

2. Select Format and choose Font.

3. To choose your typeface and type size, select a font by its number.

4. When the prompt appears, type the range you are changing and press Enter. Figure 16.1 shows the worksheet with its new font settings.

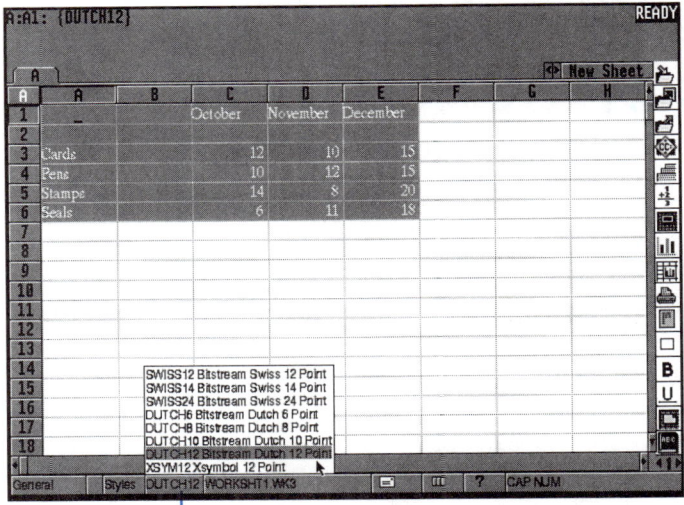

You can instantly change font styles and sizes here.

Figure 16.1　A worksheet with font settings created in Wysiwyg.

Change Default　You can change the default font at any time. Just select :Format Font Default Update, and when the Font Settings dialog box appears, select your new default font.

In the preceding steps, you saw how the colon (:) is used instead of a slash (/) to open the Wysiwyg menu. In the remainder of this book, whenever you need to open the Wysiwyg menu and select a command, the command name will begin with the colon. For instance, if you need to select Format from the Wysiwyg menu, you'll see :Format.

Adding Borders

You can lend special emphasis to particular areas of your spreadsheet if you add borders around them. Here's how:

1. Choose :Format.

2. Select Lines.

3. Select Outline.

4. At the prompt, type in the range you want to border and press Enter. The border will appear (see Figure 16.2).

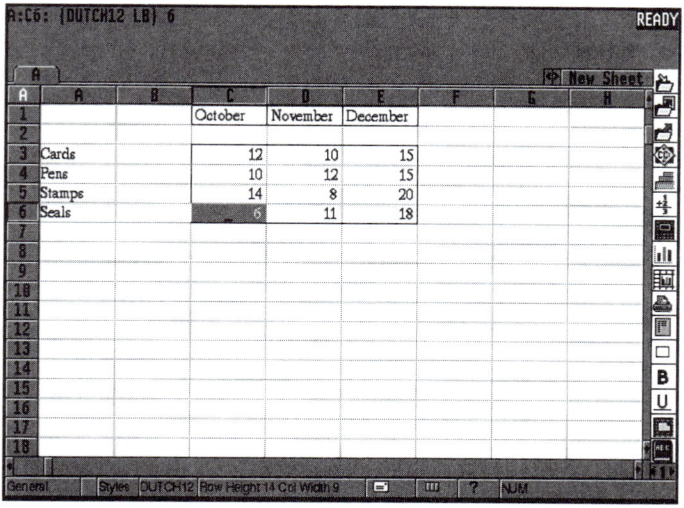

Figure 16.2 The worksheet with added borders.

Add Lines   To add lines around, underneath, to the left or right of, or above single cells, use the : Format Lines command.

Selecting Frames

With Wysiwyg, you can easily make changes to the frame that surrounds your worksheet. For example, to show a ruler, follow these steps:

1. Choose :Display.

2. Select Options.

3. Select Frame.

4. Select Special from the options that appear.

5. Select Inches. The ruler line appears at the top of the frame.

6. Select Quit two times. You are returned to READY mode.

Line Height

If you want to change the line height of your worksheet's rows, the procedure is simple. Use these steps:

1. Choose :Worksheet.

2. Select Row.

3. Select Set-Height.

4. Select the row (or range of rows) you want changed.

5. Press Enter.

6. Type in the new line height, in points.

7. Press Enter.

Turning the Grid On and Off

Using Wysiwyg, you can turn the grid lines in your worksheet on and off. To turn the grid lines on or off, follow these steps:

1. Choose :Display.

2. Select Options.

3. Select Grid.

4. Select Yes to turn on the grid lines or No to turn off the grid lines.

Using Preset Styles

Why go to a lot of extra trouble when 1-2-3 has already done the work for you? Using the Styles icon on the status bar (shown in Figure 16.3), you can instantly spruce up the look of your worksheet. Simply highlight the range you want to change, click on the Styles button on the status bar, and then click on the style you want to use. It's as simple as that. To learn what the styles look like, experiment with them all on a sample worksheet.

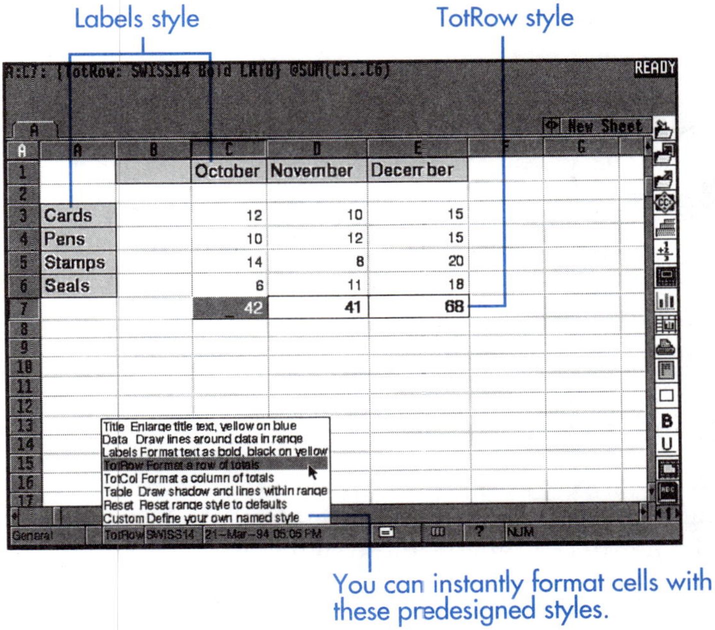

Labels style   TotRow style

You can instantly format cells with
these predesigned styles.

Figure 16.3   Using preset styles to dress up text.

In this lesson, you learned how to use some of
Wysiwyg's features. Wysiwyg has many other useful commands; refer to your 1-2-3 Reference manual to learn more
about them. In the next lesson, you will learn how to print
your worksheet.

17

Printing Worksheets

In this lesson, you will learn how to print a worksheet, add headers and footers, and print in landscape mode.

Quick Printing

When your worksheet is ready to print, you can use 1-2-3's Print commands to print your worksheet. To print a specified range of cells, follow these steps:

1. Choose /Print.

2. Choose Printer.

3. Choose Range.

4. Move to the first cell of the range you want to print. For example, press Home to move to A1 (the starting point of our example range).

5. Press . (period) to anchor the cell pointer in the first cell.

6. Move the cell pointer to the last cell of the range you want to print. For our example, move to the rightmost bottom cell on your spreadsheet.

7. Press Enter to accept the print range (in this example, A1..F16).

8. Select Align to ensure your printer will begin printing each page at the top of the paper.

9. Choose Go to begin printing. The range is printed.

10. Select Page to advance the paper to the top of the next page so that the paper will be aligned correctly the next time you need to print.

11. Select Quit to return to the worksheet.

If for any reason you need to stop the printing process, press Ctrl+Break.

> Use the Print SmartIcon from Palette 1 to print your worksheets.

Printing Options

In the previous procedure you used /Print Printer Align Go to do a quick print, accepting the default values. But as you worked through the steps, you were offered a variety of options that you could have selected. Table 17.1 gives you a look at these.

> **Need a Break?** A page break, that is! You can add one. First decide which row gets the page break, put the cell pointer in column A of that row, and then select the Page command from the Worksheet menu. The break appears at your chosen location.

Table 17.1 Print Menu Commands

Command	Enables You To
Range	Specify the range to be printed.
Line	Adjust the paper's position, line by line.

continues

Table 17.1 Continued

Command	Enables You To
Page	Move to the top of the next page.
Options	Choose different print settings and enhancements.
Clear	Remove any previous settings.
Align	Specify the present position of the paper as the page top (dot-matrix printers only).
Go	Start printing.
Quit	Exit the Print menu.

Printing Your Worksheet You can record the formulas in your worksheet by printing them out. Choose /Print Printer Options Other Cell-Formulas and then specify the print range.

Printing in Landscape Mode

Both the Wysiwyg menu and the main menu have Print commands. Printing in Wysiwyg is easier and faster because you don't have to align the paper. It automatically starts at the top of the page.

In addition to printing in *portrait mode* (across the width of the paper), Wysiwyg prints in *landscape mode* (along the length of the paper)—provided this mode is available on your printer. If it is not, 1-2-3 will display an error message when you select the :Print Go command. The path to follow is: Print Config Orientation Landscape. See Figure 17.1 for the landscape orientation option.

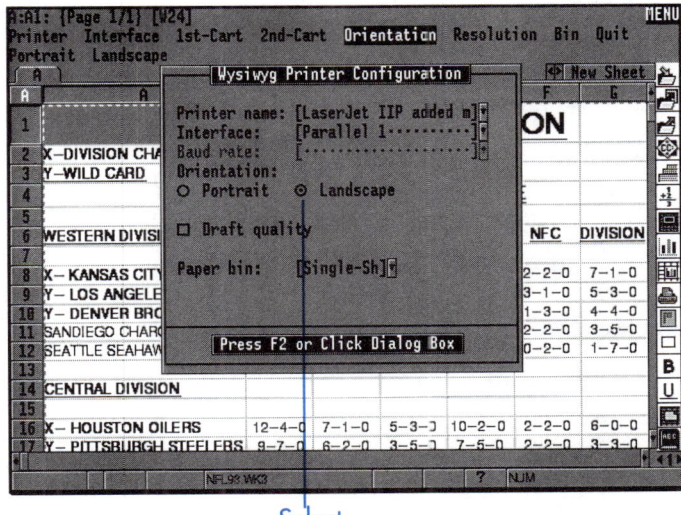

Select
Landscape

Figure 17.1   Choosing landscape orientation for printing.

Headers and Footers

When your worksheet is printed, six lines are provided automatically for headers and footers. Three of these (at the top of the page) are reserved for the header; three more at the bottom accommodate the footer.

Header   Descriptive text at the top of the printed page that is not a part of the spreadsheet itself. Headers show only when printed.

Footer   Descriptive text at the bottom of the printed page that is not a part of the spreadsheet. Footers show only when printed.

It's very easy to enter a header or footer. Here are the steps:

1. Choose /Print.

2. Select Printer.

3. Choose Range. Type in the range you want to print.

4. Select Options.

5. Select Header or Footer.

6. At the prompt, type in the text you want to appear in your header or footer (for example, the name of your company or the current date).

7. Press Enter.

8. Choose Quit once you've entered the text. The new headers and footers are stored with your worksheet, and will print.

Optional characters are also available that will put alignment information, page numbers, and dates in headers and footers. Just type these characters into the Header and Footer prompts as you would any text. See Table 17.2 for the available characters.

Table 17.2 Optional Characters Used in Headers and Footers

Character	Function
|	Centers any text that follows.
| |	Right-justifies any text that follows the second character.
#	Prints the page number at the position of the character.
@	Uses the format DD-MM-YY to print the system date.

In this lesson, you learned how to print either a whole worksheet or a screen, use landscape mode, and print headers, footers, and formulas. In the next lesson, you will learn how to graph your worksheet data.

Lesson

Graphing in Lotus 1-2-3

The next three lessons are dedicated to the art of creating, naming, saving, enhancing, and printing graphs. In this lesson, you will learn the basics: creating good-looking bar and pie graphs quickly.

Graphing Basics

You've undoubtedly heard the saying that a picture is worth a thousand words. Few people would argue the benefits of interpreting numbers by viewing graphs, as opposed to deciphering a worksheet full of numbers. Graphs show us many things about the numbers you've crunched on a worksheet. They show comparisons, trends, percentage of a whole, and progress. You'll need to know the following graphing terms:

X-axis   The left to right (horizontal) directions on a graph, usually indicating time line.

Y-axis   The bottom to top (vertical) direction on a graph, usually indicating value increment.

Legend   A separate box to the side of a graph that identifies the source of the x-axis data.

1-2-3 gives you the ability to create seven types of graphs (see Table 18.1), some familiar, some not. Yet, once you've built one type of graph, you'll see that the steps are quite similar for all types.

Table 18.1   Graph Types in 1-2-3

Type	Used to Explain
Bar	Values in two or more ranges of data. You could use a bar graph to show average grades of five classes over a semester.
Line	Trends of data, tracked over time (e.g., the grades of five students over a semester).
Pie	How values in a series compare to a whole (e.g., the percentage of A's, B's, and C's on an exam).
Stacked Bar	The role of each data item in a total. One bar might give a percentage of all students class attendance; bar segments might show the attendance percentage of each class.
XY	Relationships between different types of numbers (e.g., total student grades compared with grades of one particular class). XY graphs are also called *scattergrams*.
HLCO (High, Low, Close, Open)	Changes in one set of data over a specified period of time (e.g., the stock market over one day).
Mixed	Two different types of data in a single graph. Often comprised of a bar graph and a line graph within one boundary.

Bar Graphs

This lesson will be easier to understand if you build a small worksheet first, and use it as an example. You could create a simple worksheet, showing average classroom test scores for two groups of students, the Bluebirds and the Redbirds. Bluebird scores are: 87, 98, and 95. Redbird scores are 78, 88, and 96 (see Figure 18.1).

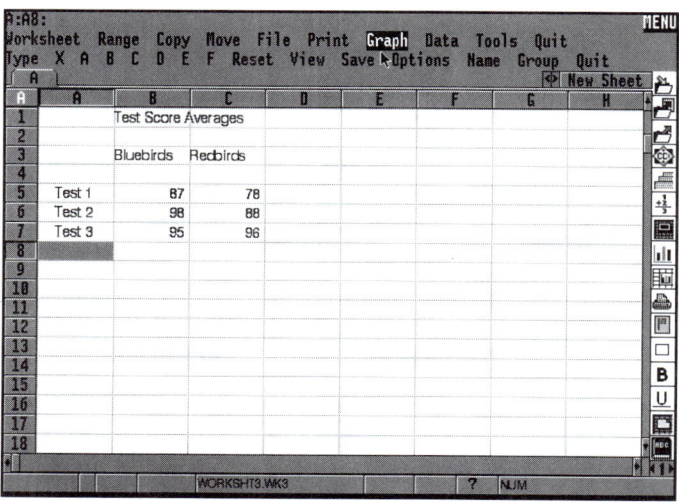

Figure 18.1 The Student Scores worksheet, with the Graph command highlighted.

Using this example, you could produce a bar graph that shows how each of the two groups in the Super Student School scores on the series of first-semester tests. Once you're ready to build a graph, here are the steps to follow:

1. Choose /Graph. The Graph Settings dialog box appears, as shown in Figure 18.2.

2. Press F2 or click on the dialog box to edit it.

3. Next to Graph Type, select Bar.

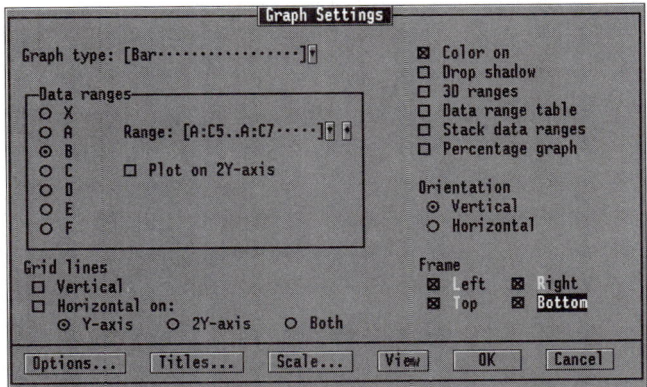

Figure 18.2   The Graph Settings dialog box.

4. Under Data Ranges, choose A as the first data range you will graph.

5. Highlight (or type in) the range; for the example, use B5..B7.

6. Select B as the second data range you will graph.

7. Select or type in the range (C5..C7 for the example).

8. Choose X.

9. Select or type in the range (A5..A7 for the example) to tell 1-2-3 which cells to use as labels along the x-axis of the graph (Test1, Test2, Test3 in this case).

10. Select the View button to see the graph you've created (see Figure 18.3).

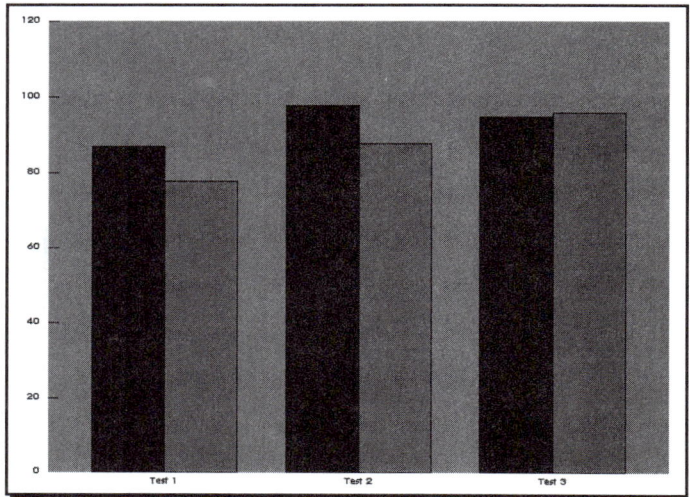

Figure 18.3   The bar graph created from the sample worksheet.

Use the Graph SmartIcon to build your graph. Select the range you want to graph, and then choose the Graph SmartIcon from palette 1 to create a quick bar graph.

Where's the Graph?   Your PC's memory (or the type of display you have) may not allow you to see your graph when you are using Wysiwyg mode. If this happens, return to the main menu (Alt+F10), select Add-In Remove Wysiwyg, and then repeat the steps to view your graph.

Remove Setting   If you have created a graph previously, you've already entered values for the X, A, and B data ranges. To enter new values for these ranges (to go with your new graph), select /Graph Reset Ranges.

Pie Graphs

Creating a sample pie graph is simple. Choose the /Graph Type command and choose Pie. Then just specify the A range (B5..B7 from the example) and an X range (A5..A7 from the example). Remember, pie charts are used to depict just one set of data.

In this lesson, you learned the types of graphs you can set up in 1-2-3. Then you learned how to create a bar and pie graph. The next lesson shows you how to dress up your graphs by adding enhancements. Then you will learn how to name and save your graphs.

Lesson

19

Enhancing Graphs

In this lesson, you'll learn how to give your graphs proper titles, legends, and names, and you'll learn how to save your graphs.

Graph Enhancements?

Enhancements are "extras" you can use to make your graph special. For example, you can:

- Add titles and subtitles.
- Create a background pattern.
- Add and customize a legend.

Give Your Graph Titles

A *title* helps the reader understand the graph's purpose. Use the bar graph you created in Lesson 18 to try the following example:

> **Before You Add a Title** Make sure to reset the Graph Type to Bar if you are using this example.

1. Choose /Graph. The Graphs Settings dialog box appears.

2. Press F2 or click on the dialog box. A Titles button appears at the bottom of the dialog box.

3. Click on the Titles button. The Titles dialog box appears. 1-2-3 gives you the option of entering titles for the first and second lines, and the x- and y-axis.

4. Next to First, type your title's first line (Test Score Averages in the example graph).

5. Next to Second, type your title's second line (First Semester in the example graph) and click on OK.

6. Press F10 to display the graph (see Figure 19.1).

7. Press Esc repeatedly to return to the worksheet.

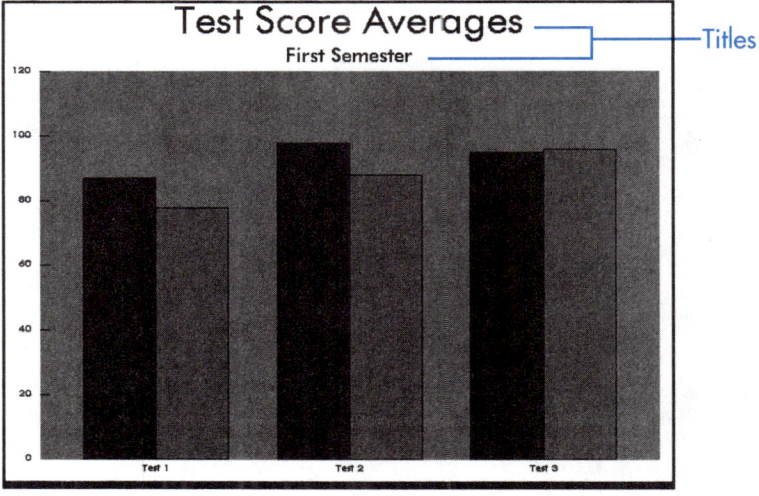

Figure 19.1   Adding titles to the sample graph.

Adding a Legend

A *legend* helps explain your graph's data by defining your data series. Here's how to add a legend:

1. Choose /Graph.

2. Choose Options. The Graph Options dialog box appears, as shown in Figure 19.2.

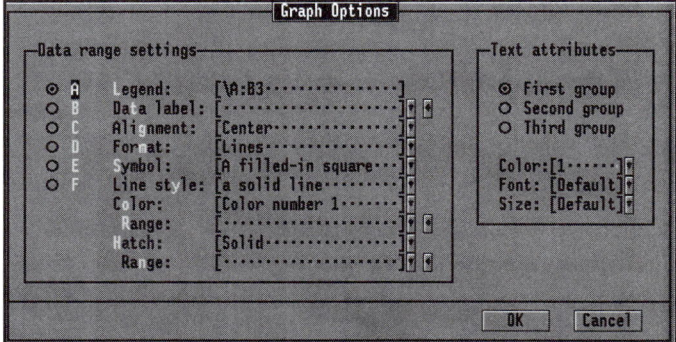

Figure 19.2   The Graph Options dialog box.

3. Choose Legend.

4. Choose A.

5. Type the address of the cell containing the label that starts your first data range (B3 in the example).

6. To add legends for other data ranges, repeat steps 3 through 6 for each one you want to add.

7. Press F10 to view your graph, complete with titles and legend (see Figure 19.3). Press Esc to return to the worksheet.

> **All Together Now**   Use the Graph Options dialog box (see Figure 19.2) to enter all your graph's text attributes, legends, symbols, line styles, colors and data labels at once. Choose the /Graph Options command to access this dialog box.

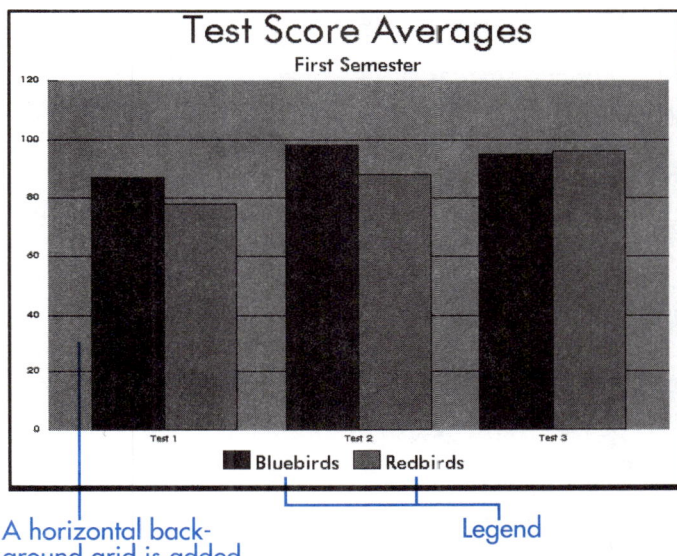

A horizontal back-
ground grid is added.

Legend

Figure 19.3 The completed worksheet with titles, legend,
and grid lines.

Setting the Graph's Background Grid

You can customize your graph further by following these
steps for adding a *background grid*. The grid adds texture to
the graph and livens up a boring chart. Follow these steps:

1. Choose /Graph. The Graph Settings dialog box
appears.

2. Press F2 or click on the dialog box.

3. Under Grid lines, select one option: Horizontal,
Vertical, Both, 2Y-axis, or Y-axis (for the example,
choose Horizontal, Y-axis).

4. To view the graph, press F10. 1-2-3 adds a grid to
the back of your graph, as shown in Figure 19.3.

Name That Graph!

You might create several graphs to accompany one worksheet. Using several graphs allows you to choose the most effective way to display the data you've gathered. When working with several graphs, you can keep them straight by naming them. Here is how to name the graph:

1. Choose /Graph.

2. Choose Name.

3. Choose Create.

4. Type the graph name and press Enter. 1-2-3 names the graph.

5. Press the Esc key until you return to the worksheet.

Saving Your Graph

Using the /Graph Save command to save your worksheet will ensure that your graph is saved with the worksheet. If you want, you can use the graph by itself, for example, in the PrintGraph program. (See your Lotus documentation for details on this program.) You can also save a graph independent of the worksheet. To do this, follow these steps:

1. Select /Graph.

2. Select Save.

3. At the **Enter graph file name:** prompt, type a name for the file.

4. Press Enter, and 1-2-3 saves the file. From here, you can access the PrintGraph program to print the graph if you want.

5. Press the Esc key until you return to the worksheet.

In this lesson, you learned how to enhance your graph by assigning titles, legends, and names. You also learned how to save a graph independently of the source worksheet. In the next lesson, you will learn how to print your current and named graphs.

Lesson 20

Printing Your Graphs

In this lesson, you will learn how to print your current graph, print a named graph, and print a graph along with worksheet data.

Printing a Current Graph

If you've developed your current graph to your satisfaction, here's how to print it.

> **Not Ready**   If you are viewing the graph, press any key to return to the READY mode before you start this procedure.

1. Select /Print.

2. Select Printer.

3. Select Align to inform 1-2-3 that the paper is positioned at the top of the page.

4. Select Image, and then choose Current.

5. Choose Go to start printing.

Printing a Named Graph

If the graph is named, you can print it without first making it the current one. Follow these steps:

1. Select /Print.

2. Select Printer.

3. Choose Image.

4. Select Named-Graph (see Figure 20.1).

5. Highlight the graph's name.

6. Press Enter.

7. Choose Go to start printing.

8. Choose Page to move the paper to the top of the next page.

9. Select Quit to return to READY mode.

Note that this procedure will not always work, depending on the size of the spreadsheet and graph.

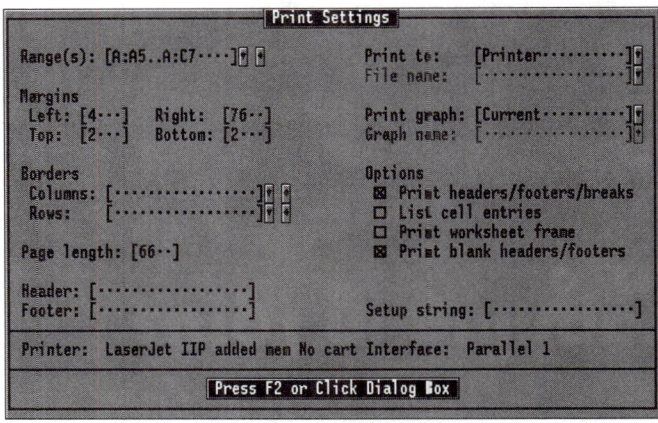

Figure 20.1   Selecting the Named-Graph option.

Printing a Graph with Worksheet Data

Here's a chance to make a dramatic presentation! Print your graph (either the current graph or a named one) with your worksheet data—on the same page.

The following steps will print your graph on the same page as your worksheet data. 1-2-3 prints the range of data first, followed by the graph. (If you want, you can reorder the steps to print the graph first.)

Printing the Worksheet Data

1. Select /Print.

2. Select Printer.

3. Choose Range.

4. Move the cell pointer to the top of the range.

5. Press . (period) to anchor the cell pointer.

6. Highlight the whole range you intend to print.

7. Press Enter to mark the end of the range.

8. Choose Go to start printing.

Printing the Graph

1. Select /Print.

2. Select Printer.

3. Choose Image to specify printing your graph.

4. Select Named-Graph to indicate a named graph.

5. Highlight the name of your designated graph.

6. Press Enter.

7. Choose Go to start printing your graph on the same page as the worksheet data.

8. Select Page to move the paper to the top of the next page.

9. Select Quit to return to READY mode. Your graph is printed on the same page as the worksheet data.

In this lesson, you learned how to print the current or named graph, and how to print a graph along with the worksheet data. In the next lesson, you will learn how to work with multiple worksheets.

Lesson

Working with Multiple Worksheets

In this lesson, you will learn how to work with multiple worksheets in one file.

Perhaps you have a group of pizza parlors and want to create a file that holds an income statement for each parlor and pulls together the data entries for each chain. If your file contains more than one worksheet, you can save a lot of time by formatting all the data at once—and by moving from one area to another with a single keystroke.

Working with more than one worksheet in a file involves these activities:

- Adding new worksheets to a file.
- Moving from one worksheet to another.
- Formatting more than one worksheet at a time.
- Copying data from one worksheet to another.
- Editing the worksheet titles.

The first step in working with multiple worksheets is to clear all active files from your screen (if they're important, save them first!), and replace them with one blank worksheet. To accomplish this, select /Worksheet and then Erase. Select Yes to clear all files from your screen and remove them from your computer's working memory. Then retrieve your first worksheet. The file is now called a *single-sheet file* because there is only one worksheet in it (but that is about to change).

Add New Worksheets

Assume that you want to add new information to your file, such as a projected income statement for a second and third pizza parlor. When more than one worksheet is in memory, you can work with any one of them—or with several at the same time. You can also move between worksheets, like flipping through pages in a notebook. A file containing more than one worksheet is called a *multiple-sheet file*.

Lotus 1-2-3 assigns letters to worksheets: the first worksheet is A, the second is B, and so on through IV. The number of worksheets you can hold in one file depends on how much memory your computer has.

The easiest way to insert a new worksheet is with the New Sheet button. Just click on the New Sheet icon at the top right side of the worksheet. A new tab appears at the top of the screen showing the new worksheet letter (see Figure 21.1). Do this several times and watch how the tabs are added at the top.

Tab for new worksheet   New Sheet button

Figure 21.1   The new worksheet is inserted after the existing one.

A New Sheet Before   To insert a new
worksheet before the current sheet, select
/Worksheet Insert Sheet Before.

Viewing Multiple Sheets at Once

To work with two worksheets at the same time, you need to
change your screen display to perspective view so that you
are able to view both worksheets at once.

1. Select /Worksheet.

2. Select Window.

3. Select Perspective.

Your screen now shows both worksheets at once, as
shown in Figure 21.2. During this process, the cell pointer
moves to the first worksheet inserted after the original,
making worksheet B the current one. You can quickly move
back and forth between worksheets by clicking on the
worksheet tabs at the top of the worksheets.

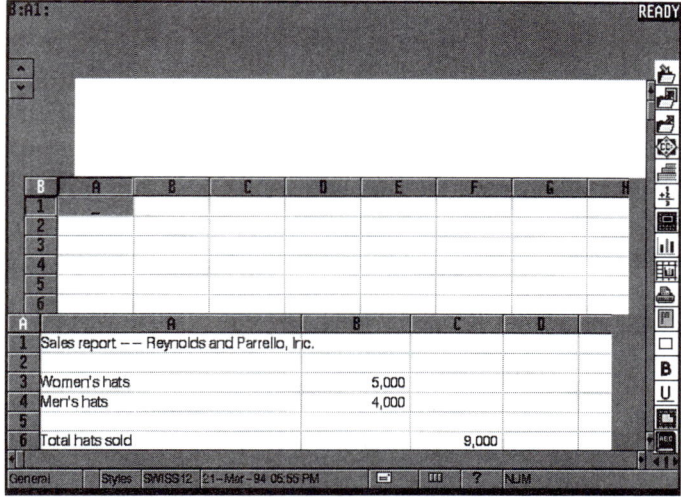

Figure 21.2   Two worksheets on-screen at once.

Quick Switch   To quickly switch between perspective view and normal view, click the Perspective View SmartIcon.

Copying Between Worksheets

You can use your main worksheet (Worksheet A) as a template or model, copying formulas and labels from it to others.

To copy the contents from worksheet A to the other(s), specify a three-dimensional range (3-D range) to copy TO. A 3-D range spans two or more consecutive worksheets in the same file.

To practice copying between worksheets, make sure you have at least 3 worksheet tabs showing—if you don't, click the New Sheet button a few times. Then follow these steps:

1. Select /Copy.

2. Move the cell pointer to highlight the contents of worksheet A.

3. Press Enter to accept the range as the range to copy FROM. Remember that for the TO range you need to specify only the upper left cell of the range, or for a 3-D range, you need to specify only the upper left cell in each worksheet in the range.

4. Press Ctrl+PgUp to move the cell pointer to B:A1.

5. Press . (period) to anchor the cell pointer in B:A1.

6. Press Ctrl+PgUp to highlight B:A1..C:A1.

7. Press Enter to accept B:A1..C:A1 as the range to copy TO.

The contents of worksheet A are copied to worksheets B and C.

Editing Worksheet Titles

You will probably want to change worksheet titles to identify what data will be stored in each. Follow these steps:

1. Press F2 (Edit) to change to EDIT mode.

2. Make the changes in text and press Enter.

3. Move to the other worksheets by pressing Ctrl+PgUp or Ctrl+PgDn.

Name your multiple-sheet file, and save it with /File Save. When you save a file while in perspective view, 1-2-3 automatically displays worksheets in perspective view the next time you retrieve the file.

In this lesson, you learned how to work with multiple worksheets. In the next lesson, you will learn how to use 1-2-3 SmartSheets.

Lesson

Using SmartSheets

In this lesson, you'll learn about 1-2-3's useful SmartSheets.

A Look at the SmartSheets

1-2-3's SmartSheets are wonderful if you use daily planners, expense reports, statements of worth, or investment records, or if you're trying to decide whether you should buy or lease a car. A *SmartSheet* is a predesigned template you can use to produce a professional looking document; you just plug in numbers and run macros that are already created. Since each SmartSheet comes complete with formulas, formatting, multiple worksheets, charts (in some), and macros, it would take you hours to create a similar file.

There are five SmartSheets available for your use. Table 22.1 gives you the file names of the SmartSheets, their titles as they appear in the worksheet, and a brief description of what each SmartSheet does for you.

Table 22.1   1-2-3 SmartSheets

File name	Worksheet title	Description
BUYLEASE.WK3	Buy vs. Lease Automobile	Helps you analyze whether you should buy or lease a car.

continues

Table 22.1   Continued

File name	Worksheet title	Description
DLYPLNNR.WK3	Daily Planner	A scheduler for organizing daily events, such as meetings, things to do, and so on.
EXPREPRT.WK3	Expense Report	Tracks meals, miles, and other expenses; includes a chart.
INVSTREC.WK3	Investment Record	A review and inventory of your current invest-ments (assets, shares, etc.). Calculates all gains and losses.
STMTWRTH.WK3	Statement of Personal Net Worth	An overview of your financial condition; includes a chart.

A Preview of the Finished Product You can take a quick look at what the finished Smart-Sheet form looks like. Open the SmartSheet and click on the Print Range SmartIcon on palette 1.

Retrieving a SmartSheet

SmartSheets are located in the 123R4D directory. You retrieve a SmartSheet the same way you retrieve any file. For example, to retrieve the Statement of Personal Net Worth SmartSheet, follow these steps from a blank worksheet:

1. Choose the /File command.

2. Choose Retrieve. A list of files appears in the Control Panel.

3. Scroll through the files until you reach STMTWRTH.WK3, and press Enter. The SmartSheet opens, as shown in Figure 22.1.

Four worksheets in one file

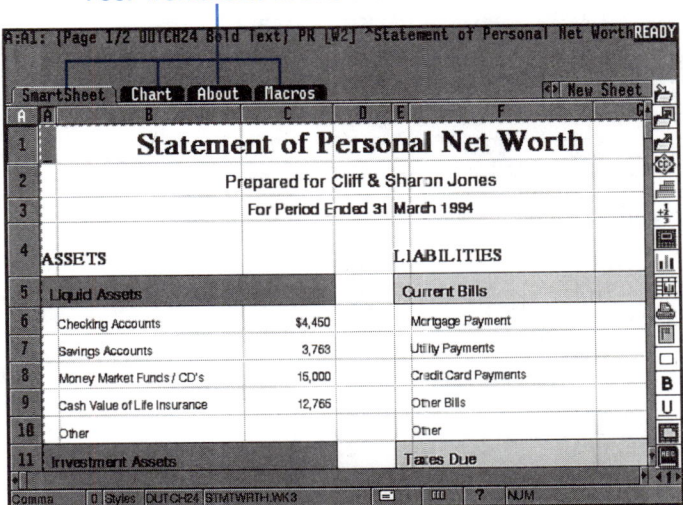

Figure 22.1 The STMTWRTH.WK3 SmartSheet.

Using the About Worksheet

Each SmartSheet contains a worksheet called "About." For instructions on how to input your own data or use the macros, and for a general description of the SmartSheet, switch to the About worksheet. Simply click on About at the top if the worksheet to move to the About worksheet (see Figure 22.2).

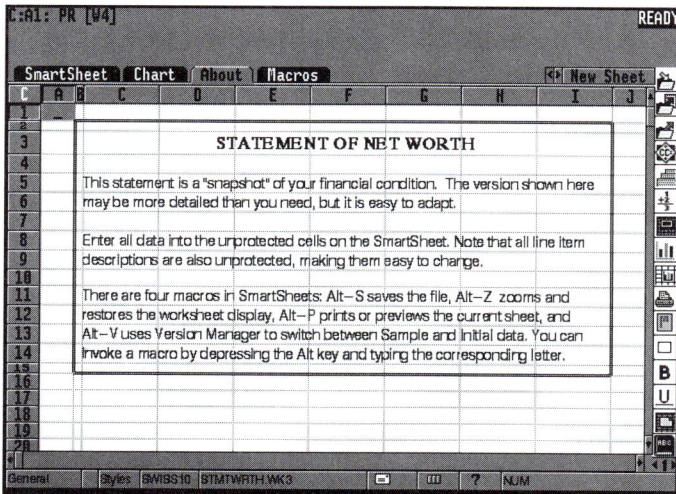

Figure 22.2 The About worksheet for STMTWRTH.WK3.

More on Macros If you want more information on the macros in a SmartSheet, click on the Macro worksheet tab to switch to the Macro worksheet. The names and code for all the macros in the SmartSheet are listed in this worksheet.

In this lesson, you learned how to use 1-2-3's SmartSheets. In the next lesson, you'll learn how to create a database.

Lesson

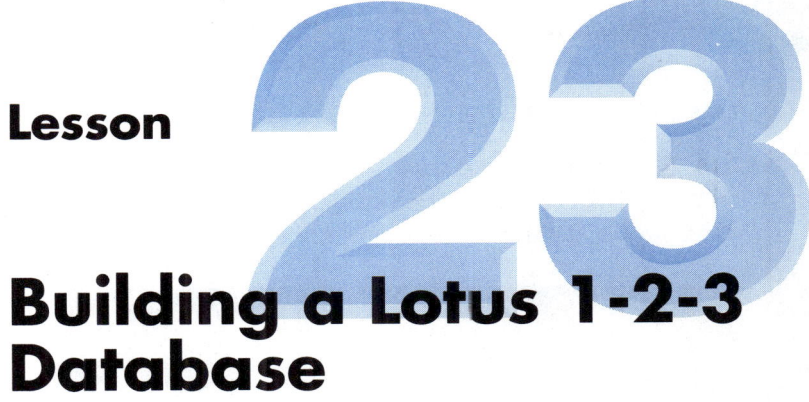

Building a Lotus 1-2-3 Database

In this lesson, you will learn how to create a database in Lotus 1-2-3.

Database Concepts

If you're new to working with databases, here are some basic terms:

- **Database** A collection of facts and figures, perhaps relating to inventory, personnel, customers, or your softball league.

- **Field** An area where you enter information such as name, age, birthday, or quantity; a field contains just one type of information for all database entries (for example, the birthday of every employee).

- **Record** A collection of all the facts and figures relating to one person or thing that are entered into fields. (The record for one employee would include that person's name, age, and birthday.)

- **Sort** To arrange records in numerical or alphabetical order.

While 1-2-3 is essentially a spreadsheet program, and not a specialized database program, you can use it to create a simple database. Storing and retrieving a number of important items (for example, clients' names, addresses, and phone numbers) can come in handy.

How the Database Works

Lotus 1-2-3's database looks (as you might expect) just like a
worksheet: rows represent records, columns represent
fields. A simple database is shown in Figure 23.1.

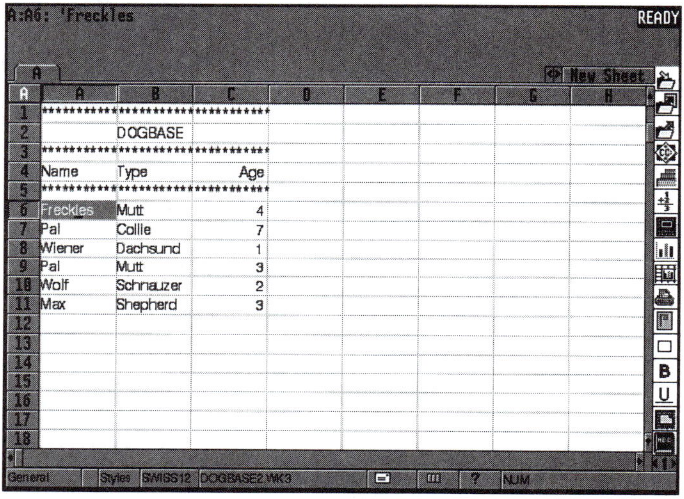

Figure 23.1 A simple 1-2-3 database, in which the rows
are records and the columns are fields.

Building Your Database

It is easy to build a 1-2-3 database, but first you need to plan
it. Think about the type of information you will need and in
what order it should appear. Write this information down on
paper before you enter your database into 1-2-3.

Enter Labels

Enter a label for a field by typing the label you want to use,
and pressing the right arrow to move to the next cell. Repeat
this step until you've entered labels for all the fields in your
database.

A Mixed Bag! Some entries contain a mix of letters and numbers. If you want an entry formatted as text so it won't be used in a calculation (for instance, a phone number), precede the entry with an apostrophe ('). This tells 1-2-3 that the entry is a text entry rather than a value.

Enter and Save Data

Once you have established the basic organization of your database, it's time to enter your records. Type the data into each cell, as displayed in Figure 23.1, and then press Enter.

Saving your database is similar to saving any other spreadsheet file. Use /File Save and name the database.

In this lesson, you learned basic database concepts and a method for using 1-2-3 to build a database. In the next lesson, you will learn how to sort records.

Lesson

Sorting Your Database

In this lesson, you will learn how to sort the data in your database.

Understanding Sorting

Data in a database begs to be organized, sorted, and re-trieved! Suppose you have 200 records, for example, names and addresses of 200 friends and family. These names would be more useful if they were alphabetized; then you need only scroll through your list to locate a particular record.

Lotus 1-2-3 allows you to choose how to sort the database by letting you designate a specific field as a "key." This *key field* can be a Lastname field, City field, or ZIP code field. You can use any of the fields in your database as a key field; in fact, you can use two key fields in the same sort.

For example, in a *two-key sort*, you can first sort on the Lastname field (as the primary field), and then sort on the Firstname field (as the secondary field). If you sort alphabeti-cally by last name and then first name and have two Joneses (a Jim Jones and a Tim Jones), Jim's name will appear on the sorted list before Tim's name.

Key Fields   Use *key fields* to designate the kind of sort operation you want to perform. To sort all the records in your database alphabeti-cally by city, for example, use the City field as the key field.

Using One Key Field for Sorting

For working through the steps in this lesson and in Lesson 25, construct the small database shown in Figure 24.1.

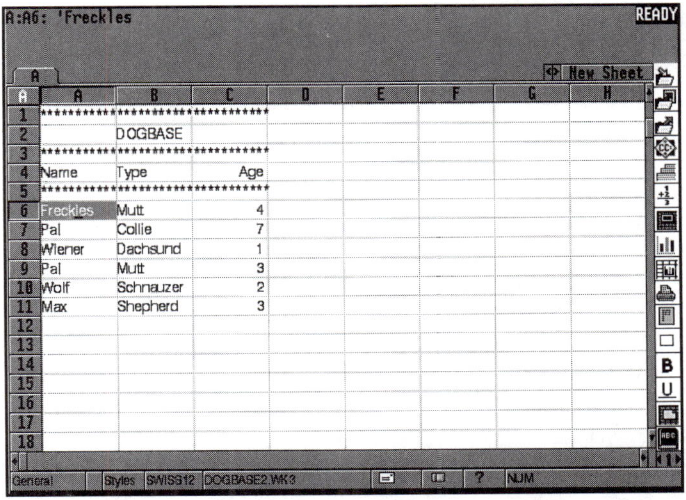

Figure 24.1   A sample unsorted database.

For this example, begin by making sure the database portion of the worksheet is on-screen (see Figure 24.1). Then alphabetize the dog records according to Name. Here are the steps for sorting these records:

1. Select /Data.

2. Choose Sort.

3. Choose Data-Range.

4. At the **Enter data range:** prompt, type in the cell addresses of the range to be sorted (or use the mouse to highlight them). Type or select only the data range to be sorted; omit the labels from this step. (For example, in this database, highlight cells A6..C11.)

5. Press Enter.

6. Select Primary-Key to choose the key field.

7. Move the cell pointer to an entry in your chosen key field. (For example, in this database, move your pointer to cell A6 and press Enter.)

8. Press A if you want to sort in Ascending order, or D to sort in Descending order. (In this example, select A.)

9. Press Enter.

10. Select Go. 1-2-3 will sort the database according to your settings.

This example alphabetizes the dog names. In the next section, you'll see how to use a secondary sort to group the dogs named Pal.

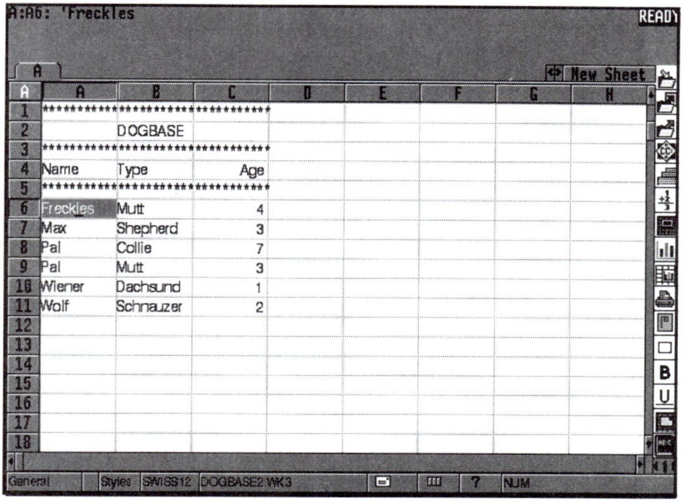

Figure 24.2 The database has been sorted by the dogs' names.

Using Two Key Fields for Sorting

You read in the earlier section of this lesson that 1-2-3 can sort on more than one key field. Try this example to sort on two key fields.

1. Select /Data.

2. Select Sort.

3. Choose Data-Range.

4. At the **Enter data range:** prompt, type in the cell addresses of the range to be sorted (or use the mouse to highlight them). Type or select only the data range to be sorted; omit the labels from this step. (For our example, type **A6..C11**.)

5. Press Enter.

6. Select Primary-Key to begin choosing the first key field.

7. Move the cell pointer to one of the entries in the field you want to designate as the first key field. (In this example, move the cell pointer to cell A6.)

8. Press Enter.

9. Select A for ascending order or D for descending order, and press Enter .(In this example, select A.)

10. Select Secondary-Key to begin choosing the second key field.

11. Move the cell pointer to one of the entries in the field you want to designate as the second key field. (For our example, choose C6.) Press Enter.

12. Indicate the sort order. (In this example, select A.)

13. Return to the Sort menu option and select Go. 1-2-3

uses your two key fields to sort the records (see Figure 24.3). Notice that the dogs named Pal are now sorted by their ages.

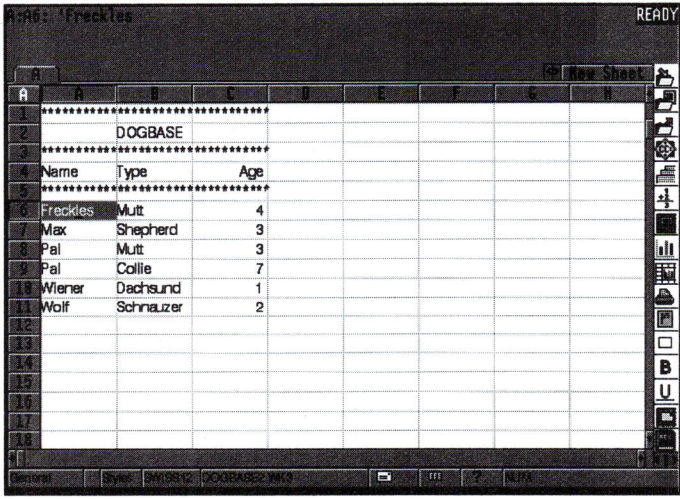

Figure 24.3 The result of the two-key sort.

In this lesson, you learned how to sort the records in your database using one and two key fields. In the final lesson, you will learn how to search for specific records.

Lesson 25

Querying Your Database

In this lesson, you will learn how to search a database for a specific record.

How Queries Work

One of the main reasons people build databases is so that they can search the database for specific records. For example, if you have a big list of names and addresses, finding all records that fall within a certain ZIP code designation can be handy.

Here are some database terms you'll need to understand, in order to work with 1-2-3's search options:

- **Data query** Specifies a record or a group of records for the database to find, and asks it to start looking.

- **Criteria range** The conditions you impose on the search, so that 1-2-3 knows which records to look for.

- **Output range** The cell range that will hold the records 1-2-3 extracts or copies from your database.

The Criteria Range

You can use the dog database that you built in the last lesson to work through this lesson. For instance, if you wanted to find all the mutts, you would need to create a *data query* that would find all the records with Mutt entered in the Type field. First, specify a *criteria range* so that 1-2-3 knows what conditions its findings have to meet. Follow these steps to create a criteria range:

1. Move the pointer to some place on the worksheet other than the database (in this example, use **A17**).

2. Type **CRITERIA RANGE** and press ↓.

3. Type the name of the field for which you want 1-2-3 to search (in this example, **Type**).

4. Press ↓.

5. Type in the specific information you want 1-2-3 to find in your designated field (for this example, type **Mutt** and press ↓). Your criteria range should look like the range in Figure 25.1.

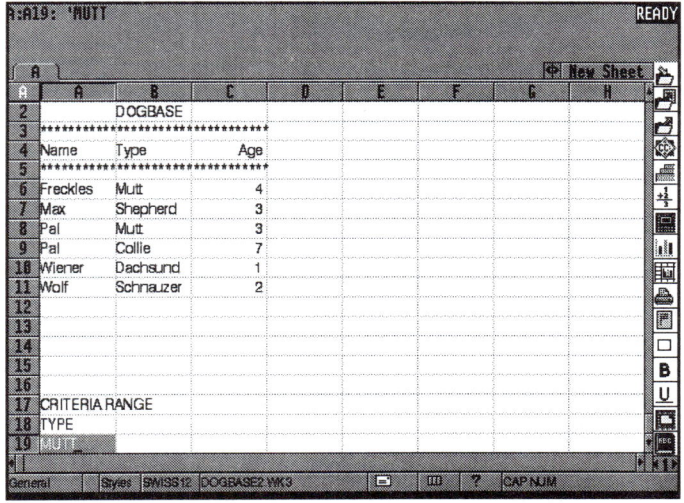

Figure 25.1 A criteria range designated for a search.

6. Select /Data Query. The Query Settings menu appears.

7. Press I, and the **Input range:** prompt appears.

8. At the prompt, type the cell addresses of the records you want to include in the search, or select them with the mouse. You can specify the entire database. (In this example, choose A4..C11 to include the field names and all data, and press Enter.)

9. Select Criteria.

10. Type the name of the range that contains the criteria field's name and data (in this example, type in A18..A19). Press Enter.

11. Choose /Find. 1-2-3 locates the first record that meets the conditions of your criteria range (see Figure 25.2).

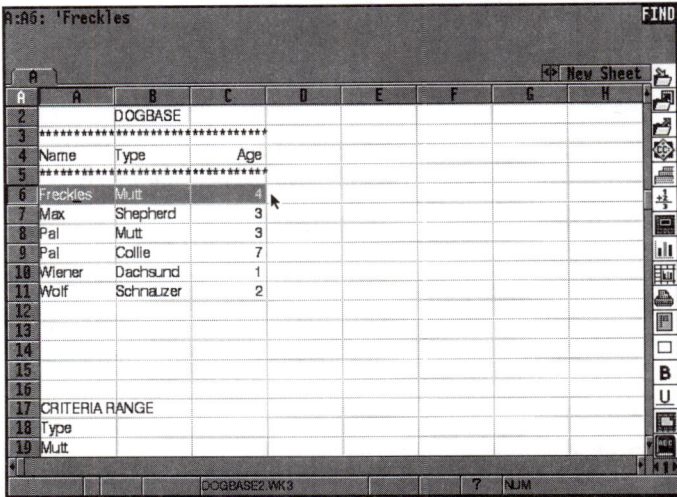

Figure 25.2   Locating records in the criteria range.

Find Next   To find additional records, press ↓ to move to the next record that meets the search criteria. Press Esc to end the search.

Extracting Records from the Database

It's possible to copy a group of records from your database, and place the copy in another range on the worksheet. The process is called *extracting* records; to do it, follow these steps:

1. Use /Copy to copy the field names (such as E4..G4) of the records you want to extract to a new location on the worksheet.

2. As you did for the /Data Query Find, select the criteria range.

3. Scroll through the records found using ↓. When you're finished, press Esc.

4. Select Output and enter a range to hold the field names you copied (in this example, E4..G4). This becomes the output range.

5. Select Extract. 1-2-3 copies all records that meet the conditions of the criteria range, and places them in the output range (see Figure 25.3).

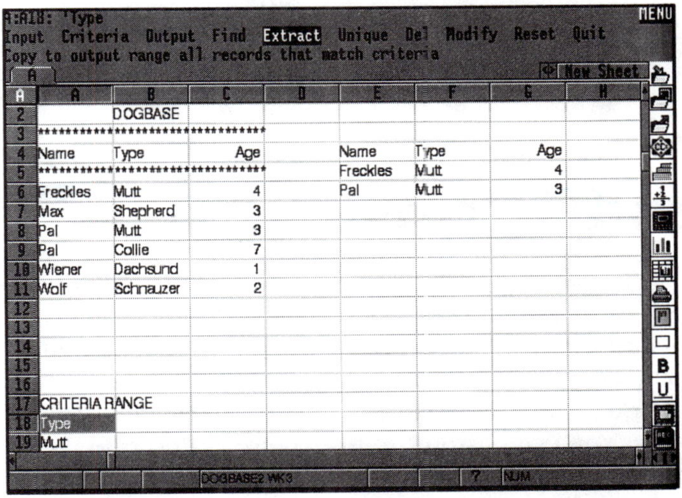

Figure 25.3 Extracted copies are recorded into the output range.

In this lesson, you learned the basics of querying your 1-2-3 database.

Appendix

SmartIcons

Palette 1

Palette 1 is the Startup, or Custom, palette. It is the palette that appears when you first start 1-2-3. It does not contain any unique icons: all of its icons are copied from other palettes. You can customize this palette as described in Lesson 5.

Icon	Function
	Saves your worksheet to a disk.
	Replaces your file with one from the disk.
	Reads a file into memory after the current file.
	Sends a message via CC:Mail.
	Shows you three worksheets, stacked up.
	Calculates the sum of values in a range.
	Accesses the Version Manager.
	Creates, edits, or displays a graph.
	Adds your graph to the worksheet.

Icon	Function
	Prints a selected range of cells.
	Previews current print range or specify/preview highlighted range.
	Cycles through available outlines and shadows.
	Adds boldface to (or removes it from) a range.
	Adds single underlining to (or removes it from) data in a range.
	Attaches a note to a cell.
	Spell checks the worksheet.

Palette 2 - Formatting

Icon	Function
	Saves your worksheet to a disk.
	Cycles through available outlines and shadows.
	Adds a drop shadow to the selected cells.
	Adds shading to the selected cells.
	Left justifies text.
	Centers text.

Icon	Function
	Right justifies text.
	Zooms the view of the worksheet.
	Cycles through available fonts.
	Cycles through available font colors.
	Cycles through available background colors.
	Adds boldface to (or removes it from) a range.
	Adds italic to (or removes it from) a range.
	Removes all text attributes from a range.
	Adds single underlining to (or removes it from) data in a range.
	Adds double underlining to (or removes it from) data in a range.

Palette 3 - Goodies

Icon	Function
	Saves your worksheet to a disk.
	Calculates the sum of values in a range.

Icon	Function
	Sums values in a range across worksheets.
	Enters today's date in the current cell or uses current date/time format.
	Starts data fill command.
	Sorts database in ascending order based on active column.
	Sorts database in descending order based on active column.
	Activates STEP mode.
	Runs a macro.
	Moves cell to a specified cell.
	Goes to last filled cell in the column.
	Goes to first filled cell in the column.
	Goes to last filled cell in the row.
	Goes to first filled cell in the row.
	Goes to upper left cell in a range.
	Goes to lower right cell in a range.

Palette 4 - Navigation

Icon	*Function*
	Saves your worksheet to a disk.
	Shows three worksheets, stacked up.
	Moves to next worksheet.
	Moves to previous worksheet.
	Moves worksheet display right one screenful.
	Moves worksheet display left one screenful.
	Moves worksheet display up one screenful.
	Moves worksheet display down one screenful.
	Moves cell pointer right one column.
	Moves cell pointer left one column.
	Moves cell pointer up one row.
	Moves cell pointer down one row.
	Moves worksheet display right one column.
	Moves worksheet display left one column.

Icon	Function
	Moves worksheet display up one row.
	Moves worksheet display down one row.

Palette 5 - Editing

Icon	Function
	Saves your worksheet to a disk.
	Replaces your file with one from the disk.
	Reads a file into memory after the current file.
	Creates a new file.
	Finds or replace characters in a range.
	Copies highlighted range to a range you specify.
	Moves highlighted range to a range you specify.
	Cancels previous action or command (if UNDO is turned on).
	Erases a range's contents.
	Copies contents of current cell to each cell in the highlighted range.
	Inserts one or more rows above selected row.

Icon	Function
	Inserts one or more columns to the left of selected column.
	Deletes all rows in the highlighted range.
	Deletes all columns in the highlighted range.
	Deletes worksheet.
	Inserts new worksheet.

Palette 6 - Publishing

Icon	Function
	Saves your worksheet to a disk.
	Formats values in a range as currency.
	Formats values in a range using comma format.
	Formats values in a range using percent format.
	Inserts page break above current row.
	Inserts page break to left of current column.
	Prints a selected range of cells.
	Previews current print range or specify/preview highlighted range.

Icon	Function
	Creates, edits, or displays a graph.
	Adds your graph to the worksheet.
	Displays current graph.
	Edits text in a selected range.
	Justifies text in a range.
	Circles highlighted cell or range.
	Copies the Wysiwyg attributes of the current range to another range.
	Recalculates all formulas in all active files.

Palette 7 - Tools

Icon	Function
	Saves your worksheet to a disk.
	Sends a message via CC:Mail.
	Accesses the Version Manager.
	Attaches a note to a cell.
	Spell checks the worksheet.

Icon	Function
	Activates STEP mode.
	Runs a macro.
	Recalculates all formulas in all active files.
	Assigns a macro to an icon.
	Adds an icon to your custom palette.
	Removes an icon from your custom palette.
	Rearranges icons in your custom palette.

Index

E

editing
  cells, 75-77
  F2 (Edit key), 60
  formulas, 60
  keys, 76
  SmartIcons (palette 5), 146-147
  worksheets, 124
Email, 55
Enter key, 35
entering
  column labels, 35
  data, 24, 131
  labels, 34-36
    databases, 130-131
    rows, 35-37
    values, 36-37
entries formatted as text, 131
Entry (control panel), 13
erasing ranges, 41-42
error messages, 2
exiting 1-2-3, 4-5
Expense Reports (SmartSheets),
  126
extracting records, 140-141

F

fields
  columns, 130
  databases, 129
  key fields, 132
  one-key field, 133-134
  two-key fields, 135-136
  two-key sort, 132
File command (main menu), 22
/File Open command, 53
/File Retrieve command, 50, 127
/File Save command, 45, 124
/File View command, 55
files
  auto backup, 48-49
  full-screen file list, 51-52

opening, 53-55
retrieving, 2-3, 24, 50
Fixed (numeric formats), 83
fonts
  default, 93
  Wysiwyg, 92-94
footers
  optional characters, 102
  printing, 101-103
format (control panel), 13
:Format Font command, 93
:Format Font Default Update
  command, 93
:Format Lines command, 95
:Format Lines Outline command, 94
formats
  automatic, 90-91
  cells, 82-84
  white space, 89-90
formatting SmartIcons (palette 2),
  143-144
formulas, 56-57
  Backsolver (add-in program),
    66-68
  building, 57-59
  cell references, 72-74
  circular references (Circs), 65-68
  editing, 60
  operators, 57-61
  parentheses, 59
  recalculating, 78-79
  Solver (add-in program), 68
Formulas command (Auditor
  menu), 64
frames (Wysiwyg), 95
full-screen file list, 51-52
function keys
  Edit key (F2), 60
  Help (F1)), 25
functions, 60-61

S

X-Y-Z

GO AHEAD. PLUG YOURSELF INTO
PRENTICE HALL COMPUTER PUBLISHING.
Introducing the PHCP Forum on CompuServe®

Yes, it's true. Now, you can have CompuServe access to the same professional, friendly folks who have made computers easier for years. On the PHCP Forum, you'll find additional information on the topics covered by every PHCP imprint—including Que, Sams Publishing, New Riders Publishing, Alpha Books, Brady Books, Hayden Books, and Adobe Press. In addition, you'll be able to receive technical support and disk updates for the software produced by Que Software and Paramount Interactive, a division of the Paramount Technology Group. It's a great way to supplement the best information in the business.

WHAT CAN YOU DO ON THE PHCP FORUM?

Play an important role in the publishing process—and make our books better while you make your work easier:

■ Leave messages and ask questions about PHCP books and software—you're guaranteed a response within 24 hours

■ Download helpful tips and software to help you get the most out of your computer

■ Contact authors of your favorite PHCP books through electronic mail

■ Present your own book ideas

■ Keep up to date on all the latest books available from each of PHCP's exciting imprints

JOIN NOW AND GET A FREE COMPUSERVE STARTER KIT!

To receive your free CompuServe Introductory Membership, call toll-free, **1-800-848-8199** and ask for representative **#597**. The Starter Kit Includes:

■ Personal ID number and password

■ $15 credit on the system

■ Subscription to CompuServe Magazine

HERE'S HOW TO PLUG INTO PHCP:

Once on the CompuServe System, type any of these phrases to access the PHCP Forum:

GO PHCP	**GO BRADY**
GO QUEBOOKS	**GO HAYDEN**
GO SAMS	**GO QUESOFT**
GO NEWRIDERS	**GO PARAMOUNTINTER**
GO ALPHA	

Once you're on the CompuServe Information Service, be sure to take advantage of all of CompuServe's resources. CompuServe is home to more than 1,700 products and services—plus it has over 1.5 million members worldwide. You'll find valuable online reference materials, travel and investor services, electronic mail, weather updates, leisure-time games and hassle-free shopping (no jam-packed parking lots or crowded stores).

Seek out the hundreds of other forums that populate CompuServe. Covering diverse topics such as pet care, rock music, cooking, and political issues, you're sure to find others with the sames concerns as you—and expand your knowledge at the same time.